6 ⁰⁰

PUEBLO CRAFTS

By
RUTH UNDERHILL
Ph. D

Originally published in 1944 by the U.S. Bureau of Indian Affairs

THE FILTER PRESS
Palmer Lake, Colorado
1979

FILTER PRESS
Wild And Woolly West BOOKS
Phone 303 481-2523

1. Choda — Thirty Pound Rails, 1956.
2. Clemens — Celebrated Jumping Frog, 1965.
3. Banks — Uncle Jim's Book of Pancakes, 1967.
4. Service — Yukon Poems, 1967.
5. Cushing — My Adventures in Zuni, 1967.
6. Englert — Oliver Perry Wiggins, 1968. *(Out of Print)*
7. Matthews — Navajo Weavers & Silversmiths, 1968.
8. Campbell — Wet Plates & Dry Gulches, 1970.
9. Banks — Alferd Packer's Wilderness Cookbook, 1969.
10. Faulk — Simple Methods of Mining Gold, 1969.
11. Rusho — Powell's Canyon Voyage, 1969.
12. Hinckley — Transcontinental Rails, 1969.
13. Young — The Grand Canyon, 1969.
14. Gehm — Nevada's Yesterdays, 1970.
15. Seig — Tobacco, Peace Pipes, & Indians, 1971.
16. Conrotto — Game Cookery Recipes, 1971.
17. Scanland — Life of Pat F. Garrett, 1971.
18. Hunt — High Country Ghost Town Poems, 1962, 1971.
19. Arpad — Buffalo Bill's Wild West, 1971.
20. Wheeler — Deadwood Dick's Leadville Lay, 1971.
21. Powell — The Hopi Villages, 1972.
22. Bathke — The West in Postage Stamps, 1973.
23. Hesse — Southwestern Indian Recipe Book, 1973.
24. Vangen — Indian Weapons, 1972.
25. MacDonald — Cockeyed Charley Parkhurst, 1973.
26. Schwatka — Among the Apaches, 1974.
27. Bourke — General Crook in the Indian Country *and*
    Remington — A Scout with the Buffalo Soldiers, 1974.
28. Powell — An Overland Trip to the Grand Canyon, 1974.
29. Harte — Luck of Roaring Camp & other sketches, 1975.
30. Remington — On the Apache Reservation & Among the Cheyennes.
31. Ferrin — Many Moons Ago, 1976.
32. Kirby — Saga of Butch Cassidy, 1977.
33. Isom — Fox Grapes, Cherokee verse, 1977.
34. Bryan — Navajo Native Dyes, 1978.
35. deBaca — Vicente Silva, Terror of Las Vegas, 1978.
36. Underhill — Pueblo Crafts, 1979.
37. Underhill — Papago & Pima Indians of Arizona, 1979.
38. Riker — Colorado Ghost Towns & Mining Camps, 1979.
39. Bennett — Genuine Navajo Weaving; How to Tell, 1979.

ISBN 0919584-51-6

904   1

PRINTED IN THE UNITED STATES OF AMERICA

WHAT THIS BOOK TELLS ABOUT
PUEBLO CRAFTS

Plate 1. Maria Martinez prepares pots

Chapter I

PUEBLO BACKGROUND

MAGINE an exhibition of pueblo crafts. On one table is a yucca ring basket made practically as it would have been a thousand years ago. On the next is a glossy black plate by Maria Martinez, one of the most famous examples of pueblo craft. Its technique was developed within the last twenty years. On the third is an embroidered "manta" from Acoma. Its diamond weave was used in the thirteenth century but the wool of its fabric was brought by the Spaniards in the seventeenth. The embroidery may have been learned then too but the red yarn, which accents its splendid dignity, was not plentiful until the railroads brought it from American cities.

Pueblo craft contains elements from all the ages and so do the pueblos themselves. A trip through these Indian villages of Arizona and New Mexico might lead us to Santa Clara on the Rio Grande with its electric lights and water hydrants. There we might see cars beside some houses and through modern glass windows we would glimpse well furnished kitchens and bedrooms. Yet the pottery sold in the market place would be in the ancient pueblo tradition and the church in the style of old Spain. A drive of less than a hundred miles would bring us to Taos, with terraced buildings out of the fourteenth century. If it were a feast day, we could see some village official in buckskins, which show that the pueblos once had much traffic with the "buffalo Indians" of the plains. Next we might jog across a desert to see the Hopi villages perched atop the once almost inaccessible Arizona mesas. On their rocky paths we could meet men in modern American dress, giving donkeys or "burros" introduced from Spain. They go to the corn fields which streak the valleys and where they cultivate varieties of maize which may date from 700 A.D.

The following study of pueblo crafts necessarily takes account of the influences which have played on these ancient villages, since their known history began in 300 A.D. It is never possible to isolate one product as in "true pueblo style," uninfluenced by whites or by other Indians. The crafts were and are living arts, developed to fill practical needs. In the course of their history, different phases of each have reached a peak, and there they have paused or dwindled until new materials, new tools, new ideas, or all three, produced a revival. Major changes usually came from the arrival of a different people. The relics show how the pueblos learned first from the south, then from the Spaniards, from the Navajo, Paiute, and Walapai, from the Plains Indians, and from White Americans.

The result was no mere copying, nor is it today. Each new resource was adjusted to the needs of pueblo life and combined with materials and ideas

Plate I-1a.   The 'D' shaped apartment house of Pueblo Bonito

Plate I-1b.   A Mesa Verde cave dwelling

already in use. Thus Indian corn, coming to the pueblos from their southern neighbors, was adapted to suit their barren plateau. The variety grown by the Hopi became so strong and drought resistant that it is used by modern agricultural experts to strengthen the taller breeds of other climates. Pueblo embroidery, some say, has been learned from the whites. Yet its most unique and beautiful color schemes come from the days when native dyes were the blue of copper sulphate, black of iron, and yellow of ochre or rabbit brush. Its designs are sometimes those of the most ancient basketry, dating more than 1500 years ago. Even watercolor painting, with the most modern of materials, achieves the serenity and jewel-like brilliance of a pueblo ceremony.

The following pages do not attempt a complete history of pueblo crafts. That would require volumes and its early stages, particularly, would lead far into archaeology. Still, we miss much light and shade of the picture as seen today, unless we know something of the materials which have gone to make it. The outline below, therefore, gives the main stages in pueblo history, only telescoping some of the earlier ones for purposes of simplicity. The dates are those established by the modern science of tree rings, first worked out in the Southwest. This means counting the rings which a tree trunk adds to its growth every year, the new wood always at the outside. In wet years the new ring is thick, in dry ones, thin or absent. The general series is the same for all trees of one kind in one general locality. It is possible, therefore, to compare logs cut at different dates and finally to establish a tree calendar, stretching back even through the first century A.D. This work has been done in the pueblo country, where students have examined thousands of old charred timbers and related them to the scraps of pottery, string and dried corn found nearby. This has resulted in some definite dates for pueblo history as outlined below.

Basketmaker Period 300-700 A.D.

This marks the first steps of the ancestors of today's pueblo Indians in agriculture, pottery, and housebuilding. It finds a people known as the Basketmakers from their principal art, scattered in a wide radius around the "Four Corners" where the modern States of Arizona, New Mexico, Colorado, and Utah meet. These people wandered about hunting and seed gathering, but they also raised small ears of corn. During the period, new influences came from the mountains at the south, where lived a people a little more advanced in the arts than the Basketmakers. These influences crept in unevenly, but in some parts of the country appeared a "permanent" house, even though it was no more than a slab-sided pit roofed over with boughs. The Basketmakers took up the idea of pottery and began to work it out for themselves, though in the style of their mountain neighbors. They improved their corn; they raised squash and a few beans.

3

Early Pueblo Period 700-1100 A.D.

In the former period, the influence from the south acted mostly at a distance. New people now arrived with their new ways and the life of the country was slowly revolutionized. The newcomers, probably from the mountainous country south of the Mogollon Rim, intermarried peacefully with the Basketmakers. The two groups, whose various ruins dot the Four Corners country, are often spoken of all together by the Navaho name Anasazi, Ancient People. They were the ancestors of the modern pueblos.

In the crowded centuries after the new arrivals, houses changed from a primitive "pit house" to clusters of rectangular rooms built of stones or poles plastered with mud. The most advanced of them were great D shaped apartment houses, like Pueblo Bonito, whose ruins are famous today. Around them were their gardens of squash and of varicolored corn, and a greater profusion of beans. A new crop, cotton, appeared, no doubt brought from the south, and the diggers surmise that there must have been some loom weaving. The art of pottery moved on to beautiful vessels, decorated in black. All the arts improved except basketry, which was being crowded out by the new inventions.

Great Pueblo Period 1100-1300 A.D.

These two hundred years mark the flowering time of the pueblos. The beauties of architecture, pottery, and weaving which had appeared only here and there spread over all pueblo country. The area covered was smaller than it had been and the villages larger. In fact, they were as near to cities as the United States Indians ever came, and "cities" the Spaniards later called them. They all made beautiful pottery and some decorated it in black, white, and red. They wove cotton fabrics on a vertical loom, such as is used today, and they developed intricate weaves. They did good work in skin and stone and jewelry and they traded their goods far and wide. Many a backload reached them in turn from southern Arizona, from the Colorado River, and even from Mexico.

Period of Resettlement and Enemy Immigration 1300-1600 A.D.

Drought put an end to the great period. For twenty-two years (1276-1298) there was almost no rain in the Southwest. The gardens, watered mostly by summer storms, withered, and the magnificent dwellings had to be abandoned. Pueblo people shifted south and east, seeking streams and springs and they resettled in locations very near those of today. The ruins of their hastily built houses show no such care and beauty as in the great period. Still they went on with crafts. The Hopi found a new method of baking pottery. The Zuni and others used a glaze. The loom blocks in the villages show how industriously they wove. Perhaps they might have worked up to a new peak of development but they were not left alone. New immigrants came in, and this time, not friendly teachers from the south. These were hunters and wanderers from the north, the Navajo, Apache, Paiute, and Walapai. Now it became the pueblos' turn to teach. The Navajo, particularly, camped near them, sometimes fighting with them but also intermarrying and learning eagerly. Today, many Navaho crafts and ceremonies are a reflection from the pueblos, though imbued with distinctly Navaho characteristics.

Spanish Period 1600-1800 A.D.

In 1598 a Spanish governor reached the Rio Grande with horses, cattle, craftsmen, and colonists, and settled down to rule the country for Spain. Previous explorations, spectacular in white history, had made little difference to pueblo life. This brought a change to every department of it, from religion to pottery. The pueblos were not all equally affected and desert villages like the Hopi kept many of their ancient forms to the twentieth century. The others, though oppressed, did much learning in new arts, while some of their older arts declined. On the side of decline, we must put the great art of pottery, which had moved upward in such a long swing. Now pots were produced in quantity for Spanish use. They came to be carelessly made and were often mere kitchen articles.

On the side of learning, agriculture came first. Up to now the Indian crops had been corn, beans and squash but the Spaniards brought wheat, fruit and several new vegetables. Pueblo people worked at the ranches and saw how wheat was irrigated, threshed with horses, and made into bread. "Officially" they themselves were not allowed to have horses, so probably they bought much of their wheat, or at least paid to have it threshed. Still they stored up the knowledge for a future time. They began to raise peaches, cabbages and peppers so that their food possibilities were practically doubled.

Housebuilding took new ideas also. The Spaniards came from adobe villages where the houses of common people were not much more luxurious than those of the pueblos. Still, they had chimneys, stairs, and "beehive" ovens. It may have been from them that the pueblos learned at least to make the last two. Perhaps, too, they learned about gypsum for whitewash and selenite for windows. Spanish missions taught knitting and embroidery. Spanish colonists brought sheep, wool carding and new dyes. Pueblos weaving became colorful and prolific, and pueblo costume took on the magnificent form it has today.

Period of Confusion 1823-1880 A.D.

In 1823 Mexico, including our Southwest, won independence from Spain. From then until the railroads came in the 1880's there was a period of confusion. During the first part of it, the pueblos were under Mexico (1823-1848), and during the last under the United States. Neither country had

5

PUEBLO OF TAOS, NEW MEXICO.

leisure to give them much attention. A few officials, soldiers, trappers, and miners were the only whites they saw. Finally a few Government schools were opened but their effects were not felt until later. This was principally a time of movement and of contact with other Indians. During Spanish rule, no white had been allowed to live inside a pueblo or within some miles of it. Now Spanish settlers moved into the fertile lands, farming on the same scale as the pueblos themselves. At this time, much more than in the previous period, pueblo people learned Spanish, and adopted some of the European peasant customs to be seen later. They soon acquired the horses and "burros" which earlier had been forbidden by the Spaniards, and they made an interesting combination by threshing wheat with horses as the Spaniards did but winnowing it with their native baskets.

Now that they had horses, they traveled more than ever. Many of them, even from as far west as the Hopi, went yearly to the Plains after buffalo. The easternmost ones, like Pecos and Taos, had constant communication with the "buffalo" Indians. Later, in the twentieth century, their grandchildren will be able to show fringed leggings, fringed shirts, and war bonnets which have been family property for generations.

At the same time the Navaho and Apache roved unchecked. There was constant fighting between them and the pueblo people, but also much neighborliness and intermarriage. Somehow, now or earlier, the combined peoples developed their peculiar moccasin, unique in the United States. Sometime after 1850 it seems that both the Navaho and the pueblos learned silver work. Some students now think that the teaching was from American Whites, though the material and many designs were from Mexico. Finally the wandering tribes were subdued by the whites (Navaho 1864, Apache in the 1880's). From this time begins the closer contact of the pueblos with the American Government.

Modern Period 1880-

In the 1880's the railroads were built through pueblo country. It is this date, much more than national allegiance, which marks the next change in craft history. Now white people flocked into the country, the Indian Bureau was more fully organized and schools were set up. More than this, there was a flood of new materials. Cheap cloth could be had in quantity so that weaving, after its long history, at last declined. Pottery slowly revived, some of it under the influence of white archaeologists. Building was modernized very quickly, except in a few towns where religious feeling prevented. There was an inrush of furniture, tools, and modern equipment. Villages near the railroad centers changed their whole aspect in a few years.

We ought, perhaps, to make another division, taking in the recent years when changes have been moving at a rate unknown before. Perhaps we

7

should begin with the pottery revival about 1910 when Maria Martinez, under the inspiration of white museum officials, began making pottery for sale in adaptations of the old styles. After that, pottery specialization in some pueblos reached the dimensions of a business. Watercolor and mural painting were taken up and developed from the barest beginnings to world famous art.

Government help went hand in hand with an economic change. In 1900 the pueblos were poor. White settlers had filled up the Rio Grande Valley so that some villages had almost no land left. Others could get no water. It was a low point for the arts, for the people drifted away to find work. Population went down and one village, Pojoaque, was practically abandoned. In 1929 a bill was passed by the Congress providing that the pueblos should be given new land or paid for what they had lost. In 1932 came a new administration, particularly interested in reviving pueblo arts and helping the villages to be self-supporting. The new funds practically revolutionized pueblo farming and of course, changed housing and daily life in many places. Still, this did not mean the death of crafts. However they were often changed to make them more suitable for sale to whites. It is uneconomical for a pueblo woman to make her own pots and baskets when she can buy cheap containers at the chain store. It is highly worth while for her to make beautiful articles as a source of income. Pottery continues, therefore, but often as a specialty of certain skilled people. Weaving was revived and so was silverwork. For the first time these crafts were taught at Government schools, by native instructors.

The following pages describe the crafts as they are today, or at least, in the modern period. However, since some of them, like stone work, died out hundreds of years ago and others, like basketry, have had such ups and downs, it seems worthwhile to glance at their past also. We should, by rights, have included agriculture, most important of all crafts, limited space prohibits. The study of pueblo crops, as well as housebuilding and costume, appears in another volume. (Workaday Life of the Pueblos)

What we must include here is some note of the differences among pueblos. A historical outline can sometimes speak of "the pueblos" as distinct from Spaniards and Navaho, though even that has to be qualified in some periods. In studying art in detail, the differences stand out strongly. They were clear enough in ancient times, when the travels of a group could be traced by the kind of pottery they made. Now, with more possibilities to choose from, each pueblo often strikes out on a different line, and sometimes more than one.

On page 17 is a list of the pueblos as they are today. It is arranged according to language groups, for the pueblos speak four different languages as well as many dialects. This is not strange when we remember how many different groups migrated to the Southwest, yet the historians cannot yet fit the migrations to the present languages. Three of these tongues are faintly related, as the list shows. They belong to a possible Aztecan-Tanoan family which stretches through much of western America and far into Mexico. Yet none of them are very much like the others of that family and they must all have been isolated so long as to form characteristics quite their own. The fourth language, Keresan, is apparently unrelated to any other Indian language and is still a bone of contention among linguists.

List of Pueblos With Their Language Groups

UTO-AZTECAN
  Hopi First Mesa
    Walpi
    Sichomovi
    Hano (Tewa language)
    Polacca
  Second Mesa
    Mishongnovi
    Shipaulovi
    Shungopovi
    Toreva
  Third Mesa
    New Oraibi
    Hotevilla (recent settlement)
    Bacabi (recent settlement)
KERESAN
  Acoma
  Laguna
  Zia
  Santa Ana
  San Felipe
  Santo Domingo
  Cochiti

TANOAN (Aztecan-Tanoan, a proposed larger family than Uto-Aztecan, taking in very distant connections.)
  Towa
    Jemez (and descendants of old Pecos)
  Tewa
    Tesuque
    Pojoaque
    Nambe
    Santa Clara
    San Ildefonso
    San Juan
  Tiwa
    Taos
    Picuris
    Sandia
    Isleta
ZUNIAN (Probably related to Uto-Aztecan)
  Zuni

The language element is important in a classification of crafts, for the speakers of one tongue can often be grouped together, as the Hopi can in weaving or the Tewa in costume. Still, geography is often as important as language. Most of the pueblos, in their present situation, are clustered in the drainage basin of the Rio Grande, New Mexico's one large river. Only a few steam off westward into the desert, like the tail of a T turned sidewise. These dwellers in a barren country find a real difference in materials and living

9

conditions from those in the river valleys. A distinction which can be made almost oftener than any other is that between desert pueblos and river pueblos.

Hopi and Zuni are the chief desert pueblos. They are nearest to the home of the ancient pueblo people, before the great drought of 1276. Perhaps they have retained more of the customs of those days. Moreover, in Spanish times, they were so far from the center of government that they were left practically alone. They had much to do with each other but little to do with the Spaniards or the river people. Especially in describing ceremonies or government, we should find that they stand out like sister villages, in contrast to all the rest. Yet two others belong partly in the desert. These are ancient Acoma, on its mesa, and Laguna, a comparatively new settlement——at least it was new in Spanish times. These belong to the Keresan language group so that they share many customs of government and ceremony different from Hopi and Zuni. Nevertheless, their situation in barren country near to the great desert pueblos seems to have cut them off somewhat from their kinsmen. In speaking of the desert pueblos, these two are included.

All the others count as river pueblos. Some, like Santo Domingo, Santa Clara and Isleta are in the fertile valley of the Rio Grande itself Some, like Jemez and Santa Ana, are on tributary creeks. Taos and Picuris are on a mountain plateau, whose tiny streams run into the youthful Rio Grande before it has tumbled into the valley. Naturally all these circumstances alter the possibilities of craft. The valley villages have much communication. They were able to get the same kind of pottery clay. They received the same amount of influence from Spaniards and from White Americans. The plateau villages, on the other hand, were near to the Plains and the buffalo hunting Indians. They were users of skins like the more eastern tribes and, moreover their climate was too cold for the raising of cotton. Their costumes were influenced as much by that of the Plains Indians as by that of their pueblo kinsmen, and so is their pottery. So are their habits of war and hunting and even of family life. In fact, it might be possible to set apart these two Tiwa villages, Taos and Picuris, as plateau pueblos, with San Juan as a transition point between them and the valley.

We could go further and further with these differences. Anyone studying the crafts of a particular pueblo will find it most absorbing to consider its sources of supply and its contacts with neighbors, past and present. These help to show how each has built up a personality which may make it stand out from a neighbor as distinctly as Boston from New Orleans. There is plenty of printed material on the subject and a glance at the classified bibliography at the end of this volume will show how varied it is. On one hand, there are the findings of the archaeologists, growing more complete every year. Again, there are the hints and descriptions to be dug out of Spanish writings. To the sorrow of the craft student, these writers were all men and usually warriors. They cared little about crafts, and a weaver puzzles her head in vain as to whether a garment described as "pintado" was really painted, embroidered, or had the pattern woven in.

In 1879 White Americans began to visit the pueblos, bringing craft work back to the National Museum in Washington. Since then, there has been a succession of reports, short and long, dealing with one detail or many. Some are now out of print and some are hard to get. It has seemed worthwhile to the Indian Bureau to have the authentic material collected, classified and brought up to date by descriptions from modern Indians. The result has been checked by experts at the Laboratory of Anthropology, Santa Fe, at the University of Mexico, the Denver Art Museum and Columbia University. The work has suggested several craft problems, noted in the various chapters. Students, white and Indian, may find them interesting subjects of study and so add to our knowledge of pueblo activities.

A companion volume, "Workaday Life of the Pueblos," also published by the Division of Education, Bureau of Indian Affairs, presents a similar panorama of their material culture. The following chapter headings indicate its contents:

WHO ARE THE PUEBLO INDIANS?
    I   Pueblo People

WHAT DID THEY EAT?
    II   Cultivated Crops, Storage and Cookery
    III   Wild Crops and How They Were Used
    IV   Hunting the Meat Supply

HOW DID THEY FIND SHELTER AND CLOTHING?
    V   Houses and Furnishings
    VI   Clothing and Style Changes

WHAT WAS THEIR DAILY LIFE?
    VII   Life in the Village, Games, Trade, War
    VIII   Life in the Family, Birth, Childhood, Boy and Girl, Marriage, Death

WHAT IS THEIR LIFE TODAY?
    IX   The Pueblos Today

Chapter II

BASKETRY

N their early days pueblo people made so much equipment from basketry materials that the first explorers called them the Basketmakers. Their product ranged from fringed skirts and sandals, through soft grass bags and stiff containers, to the house of poles and brush itself.

Then they took up pottery. They settled down, so it was safe to use breakable dishes and they no longer used baskets for cookery and storage. Even their house building was more like pottery than basketry. They began weaving and their clothes and bags were made of cloth. They let basketry die out, until at present only the Hopi make decorative baskets and then only in certain villages. Hopi, Zuni, Jemez and a few others make tough, useful baskets. But, taken all in all, the pueblos are basketmakers no longer. Styles have changed in this as in so many other things.

Yet, looking through the equipment of a pueblo, you find basketry methods in the most unexpected places —the chimney foundation, the cradle, the container for the bride's new clothes! There must be old memories of basketmaking days which have preserved these simple conveniences. Women—for they were the basketmakers —did not drop their old craft all at once. They tried a new method, like wickerwork, dropped an old one, like coiling, took coiling up again. In the course of their changing styles, they used all the main methods of basketry known to Indians of the United States.

Wickerwork.   The simplest of these is wickerwork, which is merely the weaving in and out of stiff twigs, over and under one another; it is like cloth weaving except that cloth needs a loom and wickerwork is done with fingers. The ancient house of poles and brush was wickerwork. The little brush windbreaks in the fields were wickerwork and they are still. Even in a clay or stone house, the support for the chimney hood may be wicker. The Hopi of the First and Third Mesa used wickerwork for the baby's cradle board. This is a bow of green wood with tough sumac stems tied across it with yucca or buckskin thongs. It is a specialty of the Hopi, for most of the other pueblos make their cradles from wood.

Almost all of them made a carrying basket in wickerwork. This deep container (Plate II-1) had a foundation of tough twigs of sumac (Rhus trilobata) or barberry (Berberis fendleri) tied together in star shape. Other peeled twigs were woven across them, generally over two and under two. The twigs might be fine, making a close woven basket, or coarse, making an openwork one, good for carrying corn cobs or peaches. A buckskin carrying strap was tied through the wickerwork, as in the illustration. A man coming home from the field carried this basket on his back, with the strap across his

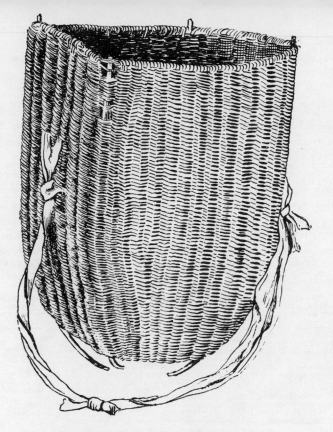

Plate II-1. Wicker basket for carrying fruit (Hopi)

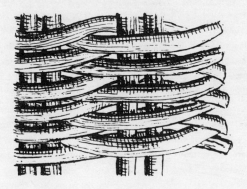

Plate II-2. Detail of wicker basket weave

13

forehead. Tradition says that, since men used the basket so much it was often they who made it, rather than the women. Such baskets are still made by the Hopi men and women and they were made at Zuni until a short time ago. Perhaps a few other pueblos weave them now and then.

Between 1200 and 1300 A.D. the Hopi began to use wickerwork for the beautiful colored trays, still made on Third Mesa. The material is sumac (Rhus trilobata) or rabbit brush of several kinds (Chrysothamnus graveolens, Bigelovia graveolens, Verbesina enceloides). The stems are peeled, rubbed with sandstone to remove irregularities and some of them are dyed. To make the tray, a number of twigs are tied together like the ribs of an umbrella and others woven across them over one, under one (Plates II-3, 4, 5), new ribs being added as the disk grows. When the edge of the tray is reached, the ends of the ribs are bent over and the rim finished with a spiral sewing of yucca leaf.

The pattern on these trays is so colorful and striking that some students have called it the most artistic basketry made in the United States. The figures represent birds or perhaps the dancing gods who visit the mesas to bring rain. Usually they are made by weaving in dyed twigs, but sometimes they are painted on the finished basket, or parts of them are painted. The colors used were originally vegetable dyes and earth colors. Then, for a time, the Hopi took to commercial aniline colors, just as blanket weavers did. Now they are using the lovely old colors again with new vegetable dyes added. Their baskets have a large sale with the whites and are popular on the mesas too, as anyone would know who has seen the brilliant trays thrown in the air at the women's Basket Dance, when the young men scramble for them.

Basketry Coloring of Second Mesa

Earth Colors. The clay or rock is ground on a small flat stone, then mixed with an oil made by chewing squash seeds. The paint is put on the twigs with a bit of fur or a rabbit foot, either before or after they have been woven into the basket.

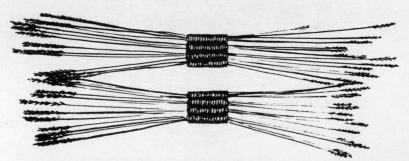

Plate II-3. Foundation of Hopi Third Mesa wicker tray

14

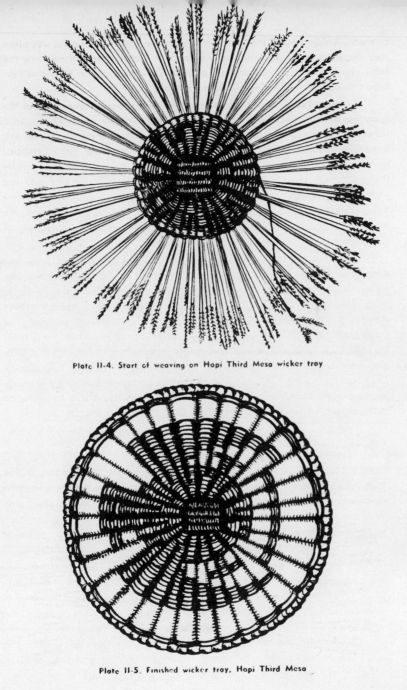

Plate II-4. Start of weaving on Hopi Third Mesa wicker tray

Plate II-5. Finished wicker tray, Hopi Third Mesa

15

White: Kaolin
Black: Soot or Coal
Green: Copper Carbonate
Red, Brown, Yellow: Iron ochres

Vegetable Colors: These are made by boiling the roots, bark or flowers mentioned and then dipping the basketry twigs in the solution. To set the dye, the twigs are sometimes held in the smoke of burning wool, white for light colors, black for darker ones.

Black:	Navy bean, Sunflower (Helianthus petiolaris) seed smoked over black wool.
Dark Blue:	The above used in weaker solution.
Light Blue:	Larkspur (Delphinium scaposum) or indigo.
Purple:	Purple corn, amaranth (armaranthus plameri).
Pink:	Amaranth (Amaranthus plameri), Cockscomb. (Varying intensities of the cockscomb dye give carmine, lavender).
Red:	Alder (Alnus tenuifolia) bark; sumac (Rhus trilobata) berries; Cockscomb, flowers.
Red Brown:	A grass, (Thelesperma gracile), boiled, strained, native alum added.
Yellow:	The yellow composite flowers, many of which are known as rabbit brush. The most common are: Chrysothamnus graveolens, Ch. bigelovii, Howardii, pinifolius.
Orange Yellow:	Saffron (Carthamus tinctorius), flowers.
Green:	Blue dye and yellow mixed. Sometimes the bark of rabbit brush.

Plaiting.   Plaiting is very like wickerwork and, in fact, the two are sometimes spoken of together as basket weaving. The difference is that wickerwork is done with stiff twigs, while plaiting uses reeds or grasses which may be quite flexible. Finer work can be done by this method and there is more chance for variations.

Long ago pueblo people used this method for their beautifully woven sandals which were given up when moccasins came in. They used it for floor mats also and those floor mats were in use, at least with the Hopi, until a short time ago. They were made of cattails or of the long tough leaves of the yucca (yucca angustifolia) split and kept moist by burying in wet sand so that they would handle easily. The weaver began in the center of the mat, laying three strips down parallel and three others across them at right angles. Then she wove in more strands in each direction, passing them over three, under three, or possibly over two, under two. This process, which gives a look of

16

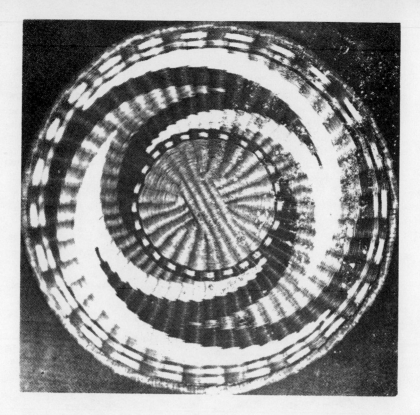

Plate II-6. Whirlwind design, vegetable dye, wicker tray, Hopi Third Mesa

slanting lines to the whole product, is called twilling and we shall meet it again in weaving.

The edge of the twilled mat was neatly finished, so that no ends showed. When the mat maker had almost reached the edge she cut off every other one of the cattail strands at that point. She plaited the remaining ones together for two or three inches, then turned them down at an angle and plaited back toward the mat, making a double border whose diagonals, on one side, ran at a different angle from those of the mat. When the plaiting reached the mat proper, she could tuck the last ends under these diagonals.

The sketch (II-7) shows one of these common plaited mats, but, as it happens, this time with a wicker border. Other articles made in plaited work were a bandage-shaped ring, about three inches wide and five or six in diameter, which a woman might place on her head or on the floor to support the bottom of a pot. Half of such a ring, a little larger, served as an awning

17

Plate II-7. Plaited mat of yucca

for the baby's cradle. There were also pack straps and the wide belt used with the waist loom. Sometimes the support for the plaster chimney hood was made of carefully plaited yucca strands instead of wickerwork.

The most popular plaited article was the wide, shallow tray used for winnowing. All the pueblos once made this tray and many do so still. Particularly at Jemez, the women say that they cannot get anything at the white store that will do as well.

A basket tray is started just like a mat but of finer materials. The yucca leaves are split into narrow widths and the sharp edges peeled off. They are woven into a square mat, with diameter a little greater than the basket is to have. When the size is right, the women wets her finished mat and pounds it with a stone to soften the yucca and make it bend easily. (II-8 and 9)

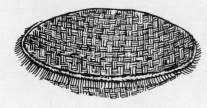

Plate II-8. Yucca ring basket, after the ring has been placed around the edge

She has already made the ring which will bind the edge of the basket. It is a long sumac rod, peeled, wet, bent into a circle and tied that way to keep its shape. She slips it under the mat, then stands on the mat and pulls its edges up until they come within the ring and the mat has the shape of a shallow bowl. The ends of the mat stand up straight inside above the ring, high at the corners and a little lower at the sides. She bends them down toward the outside over the ring and binds them with strands of split yucca leaf which have been soaking in water to make them flexible. Then she clips the ragged edge even.

Plate II-9. Softening leaves of yucca mat used in making ring basket

With this same technique she can make circular baskets of any depth, by weaving a larger mat and pushing it down deeper within the ring. Pueblo women used to make nests of such baskets in varying sizes, like the modern housewife's nest of kitchen bowls.

Twining.   Twining was another old method of Basketmaker days, now almost gone. It means that two strands at a time are woven in and out through a set of foundation strands, one passing over and one under, twisting together each time they meet. Beautiful sandals were once made by this method, so fine that they looked like cloth. Rabbitskin blankets were twined too and it is only for convenience that we describe them later under weaving, instead of here. Perhaps indeed it was the coming of weaving that put an

19

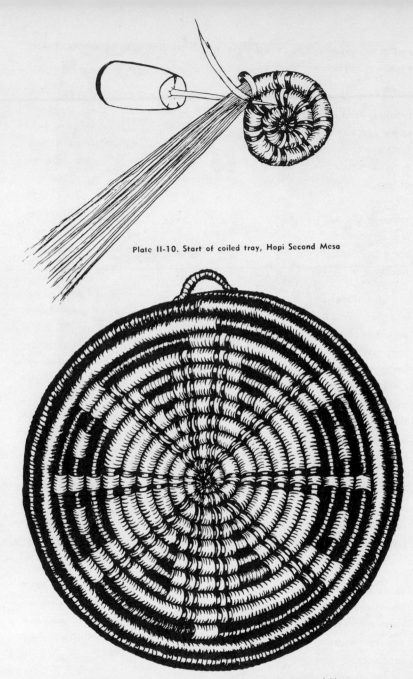

Plate II-10. Start of coiled tray, Hopi Second Mesa

Plate II-11. Finished coiled tray, natural colors, Hopi Second Mesa

end to twining, which was the ancient way of combining soft materials before there was any loom.

The only relics of it now in pueblo basketry are an occasional windbreak, a reed mat, or a door curtain. The windbreaks are rows of slender poles, placed upright, with yucca strands twined between them. The reed mats and door curtains are really the same thing, used for different purposes. A row of reeds is laid parallel in the shape of a curtain. Then two twinings of yucca string or cotton string are made at intervals down their length so that the reeds are held together like the bamboo curtains bought in modern stores. If the curtain is not too large, it can be rolled up and tied with windings of string. In that shape it forms the "suitcase" which used to be taken home by a Hopi bride after her husband's relatives had woven her wedding trousseau.

Coiling. Coiling was an old Basketmaker method, given up for awhile and then brought back by the Hopi about 1300 A.D., the great Pueblo period. No one but the Hopi uses it now and they only on Second Mesa. What they make for themselves are small basketry trays to be carried in procession and given away at the women's dance, and larger ones in which a bride carries cornmeal to her husband's house. Coiling is a little like sewing with stiff materials. The foundation is a spiral coil of twigs or grass (the Hopi use a bundle of coarse galleta grass as thick as a finger). The rounds of the coil are bound together by strips of yucca which have to be poked through the grass bundles with an awl. (Plate II-10) The Hopi lay these binding strips so close together that none of the foundation can be seen, and since many of them are colored the result is a pattern. It often represents a bird or a dancing god, as the wickerwork plaques of Third Mesa do, but here, where all the lines go around in circles instead of spreading out like sun rays, the designs have a different quality. (II-11)

The colors too are different, for Second Mesa often uses the natural tones of the yucca which come in many different shades. The tender, inside shoots are white, the new outside ones are green. The old outside ones, exposed to the sun, are yellow (or the Basketmaker may dry them artificially outside her house). She adds very little to this soft natural combination except accents of brown and black, which are colored with thelesperma grass or sunflower seeds like the wickerwork.

21

Chapter III

WEAVING

Preparing the Yarn

STRING.   Weaving is an art very much like basketry and sometimes the two use the same methods. The main difference is that a basketmaker works mostly with stiff materials, while the weaver uses flexible string or yarn. This does not mean mere fibre, whether in one strand or many. It means two or more strands of fibre twisted together, for strength. Package twine, sewing silk, and heavy rope are all made of twisted strands and so was the string made by early peoples, all over the world. String, in fact, must have been one of the first inventions and one wonders how any people got along without this way of fastening things together.

The Basketmakers made string from yucca fibre, milkweed, Indian hemp, and cedar bark. Yucca fibre was the commonest. They would wet the leaves, stems or bark, pound them up between two stones, and pull out the fibres. Then the man, who was probably the weaver even then, would lay two of these against his bare right thigh and roll them down with the palm of his right hand to twist the strands and then back to twist them together. For coarse string, or for the weaving of rabbitskin blankets to be described later, a very little twisting was enough. For stronger and finer string, the twist must be tighter. Sometimes he took two already twisted strings and rolled them together, thus making a four-ply strand. For specially good string, he used some of his wife's long hair. The looks of Basketmaker mummies convince the diggers that it was women who gave up their hair for ropemaking and not men. Now and then, buffalo or dog hair was available also but that was short and needed much rolling and matting.

Twined Weaving. Pueblo people used this homemade string until the railroads came. They still make some. They needed it for snares, nets, belts, and fastening. They also combined it with fibres, stiff or soft, and made bags, sandals, and straps which looked almost like heavy cloth. They were hardly that, for they were not made on a loom and they were done by the old basketry method of twining (see page 27) in which **two** strands are worked in and out with the fingers across another set of strands, and twined together at every intersection. (True weaving, as we shall see later, requires only one cross strand and no twining.)

Then came the next step which brought them to the very threshold of weaving. They made string out of fur or feathers and twined it with yucca cord into the blankets, (Plate III-1) which were used almost up to modern times. The work was done with the fingers, as basketry is, and there was no mechanical arrangement for separating the threads such as we shall describe

22

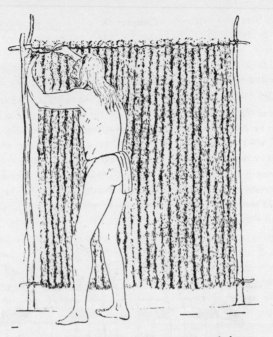

Plate III-1. Twining a rabbitskin blanket with vertical warp

later as being necessary in a loom. So this process, which made a loose, net-like fabric, is sometimes called finger weaving.

Fur Blankets. The foundation strands were made from a rope of fur or feathers which might be fifty feet long. If it was fur, it was made by cutting skins of rabbits or other small animals into strips about a quarter inch wide and wrapping these about a yucca cord so that the beginning of each one overlapped the end of the one before it. If the skins were twisted on when wet, they would dry in that position as firmly as if they were sewed. This would make a rope about half an inch thick but often it was made even thicker by doubling it and twisting two ropes together as string was twisted. If the rope was to be of feathers, the worker took the downy feathers from a turkey's breast, split them and cut off the long quill end, leaving about half an inch of flexible quill which would curl when wet as a dandelion stem curls. He curled this around the yucca cord, so that it fastened down the end of the first and so on. This feather rope was just as thick and soft as the fur rope but weighed much less.

To make the rope into a blanket, the weaver looped it back and forth across two bars spaced the width of a blanket apart. Readers of "The Northern Paiute Indians" will remember that they, too, made this blanket and that

23

their two bars were often the opposite sides of a large wooden frame, standing upright or supported on the ground. Pueblo people may sometimes have had such frames or they may have lashed the bars to floor and ceiling. Bars have actually been found in the ruins, with cords of some sort looped across them and knotted fast. Often, too, they may have used only one bar and let the loops hang free, a method which weavers testify is very convenient when passing long twining cords around them.

We shall call these foundation strands by the regular weaver's term, "warp," which means a set of strands held firmly in place while another set of movable strands is passed through them. The movable strands are known as weft, or woof. These are old English words, as are most of the terms of weaving, come down from the days when English people wove their own wool on homemade looms. The Anasazi weft was yucca string, in twined rows, spaced rather far apart. The diagram (III-2) shows how this was done

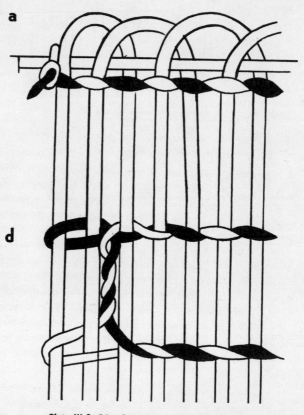

Plate III-2. Edge finish for a rabbitskin blanket

in one old fur blanket, found in a cave of northeastern Arizona. The upright warp strands, which represent the fur or feather ropes, are looped over a bar and placed farther apart than they would really be, for clearness. The twined weft begins at **a**, where it is tied, and is composed of two strands, one colored white for clearness, and the other black. The two strands pass across the blanket to a point outside the diagram, then turn and come back in another row of twining some distance below the first. The arrangement at **b** shows how this turn is made. The black weft strand loops over two warps instead of one, then comes back and twists with the white strand. The twist lies parallel with the warps for a little way, then the white strand loops over two warps and comes back to twine with the black strand across the blanket again. This makes the edge of the blanket particularly strong. Another way to do this was to wrap an extra weft strand over the two outermost warps all the way down their length in a series of loops like a buttonhole stitch in sewing. Probably there were many other ways for strengthening the edge and each weaver suited himself.

The result was quite worthy to be called a blanket. Yet the pueblos could not go on to other blankets, with firmer fabric and finer threads, until they had a mechanical invention, the loom. It is an interesting fact that the true loom, in America, arrived hand in hand with cotton. Indians in many parts of the continent had finger weaving with dog hair, mountain goat hair, buffalo hair, and vegetable fibres but (except just possibly with the Cherokee) they did not get a real loom until they got cotton and they did not get cotton without the loom.

Cotton. The first cotton garment found in ruins anywhere in the pueblos dates, by the tree rings, 795 A.D. That is all we know about when cotton arrived. We know that it was not the same as that grown in the Old World but a special New World species, named after the Hopi, Gossypium hopi. Cotton of this same species was grown from Peru up to the pueblos, that is throughout the most civilized part of America. Usually it flourished in hot, low place, just as we see it today. Only the pueblos, in their high country with its cold winters, had worked out a variety which would ripen in one hundred days, the shortest season known. Here is another proof of their skill in farming and their long experience. According to Spanish accounts, they raised cotton as far north as Cochiti, while northern Tewa and Tiwa wore skins, as did Pecos near the buffalo plains. Often they had only very small patches, for cotton needs water and they either had to manage a little irrigation or water it by hand.

As the railroads came in bringing cheap cotton cloth, the villages gave up their fields, one by one. Even the most famous of the Hopi cotton fields were turned to other crops, although they are still called Moenkopi, The Place Where Cotton Is Grown. The Hopi, almost the only weavers left, continue to raise a little cotton in small patches while an occasional weaver in some of the other pueblos may grow a little for his own use. More often, he gets it from the Hopi, paying for it with turquoise, the ancient pueblo article of trade.

Preparation of Cotton. Pueblo people harvested their cotton just as they did beans, often bringing in the whole mass, stems, pods, and all, drying it on the roof and then beating the pods loose. After the pods were separated from the stems, the fluff was pulled out by hand. Next it needed ginning (to take out the seeds). The white man does this by machinery, but pueblo people spread the fluff on a flooring of clean sand, and several of them squatted around it, each holding two or three long, pliant sticks, tied together in the shape of a switch. With these, they beat the fluff gently and tirelessly for hours, picking out the seeds as they fell away from it. Sometimes they merely pulled the cotton out by hand into long streamers, picking seeds and dirt out of each streamer with the fingers. This was a long task and often the weavers left it for the winter days when they would have time to work indoors.

If the cotton was to be used for ceremonial purposes, even this cleaning work was a ceremony. Some of the Hopi did the work in the kiva, praying over the sand as they spread it on the kiva floor. Before they brought in the cotton, they brought a painting of the sun, on deerskin, which they laid on the sand for a moment and sprinkled with cornmeal. When this was taken away, the cotton was laid on the place which it had blessed.

The Zuni, say some, had an ingenious device for ginning, which anyone who has tried to brush fluff from clothes may appreciate. They laid the cotton fluff between two woven blankets, then beat the outside of the blankets with a stick. The fibres stuck to the blanket while the seeds shook loose.

However the ginning was done, it left a mass of disordered fluff. Men pulled this roughly into hanks with their hands or perhaps with a coarse wooden comb with two or three teeth. Then they tied up the hanks and left them to be spun. Evidently they cleaned and ginned just enough for one spinning at a time, for no stores of hanks are found in the ruins.

Spinning. Next came the work of twisting the cotton into thread, or spinning. When they twisted yucca fibre, the pueblo men had rolled it along the leg with the palm of the hand. They twisted cotton with a spindle. (**d, e** and **f** in Plate III-3) This was a slender stick, about eighteen inches long, tapered at both ends and passed through a disk of wood, stone, horn, pottery, or dried squash rind. This disk, or whorl (another old English word) was about three inches in diameter. The illustration shows it about two thirds of the way down the stick, though it might be lower. It fitted the stick tightly so that it would not revolve without moving the whole spindle and often it was further secured by a winding of string above and below it.

26

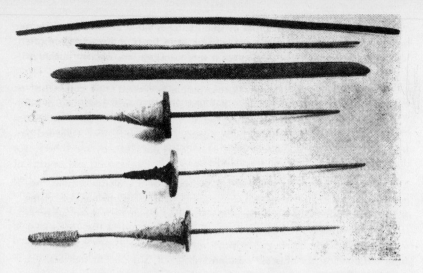

Plate III-3. Ancient spindles and battens

There were two ways of using the spindle. (Illustrated by figures III-4, 5, and 6) The first, still used by the Hopi, reminds us of the ancient method of palm on thigh. It is illustrated in figure III-4. The spinner, usually a man at Hopi, sits with a pile of cotton fluff on the floor at his left. In his right he holds the spindle, with the whorl pointing inward. He attaches a streamer of cotton to the spindle below the whorl, by winding the end around tightly a few times. Then he holds the spindle horizontally on his right thigh, under the palm of his hand. His left hand holds the streamer of cotton which can be pulled out from the fluff in one loose, continuous mass. He brings it up between the little finger and third finger of his left hand, winds it two or three times around all four fingers for firmness, then holds the hand as far up as he can so that there is a long, tight stretch of fluff between spindle and hand.

Now he starts revolving the spindle. He rolls it forward along his leg, with the palm of his hand which lies over its longer portion above the whorl. When it reaches his knee, he pulls it lightly back with thumb and middle finger and rolls it down again. More and more cotton is pulled away from his left hand and wraps itself around the spindle while the revolving motion twists the loose streamer into a fluffy cotton yarn. Meantime the left hand holds the cotton taut for it is this pull between hands and spindle that makes the twist firm.

Finally the laps of cotton are all off the left hand and it is time to pull more from the mass. Before doing this, the Hopi spinner evens the twist in the yarn he is already holding. He places the spindle under his foot as in III-6. Then he grasps the taut yarn with his right hand and reaches with his left as far as he can along the unspun thread. Then his right hand pushes the twist up along this thread. The old Hopi in the photograph has just finished this operation and has brought his right hand up to his left along an uneven twist of black wool yarn. The picture shows that a first spinning, even with these precautions, gives very irregular results. The old man may spin his wool two or three times more before using it. Meantime, to complete the first spinning, he will pull more material from the pile at his left side, wind it around his left hand and roll the spindle as before.

Hopi spinners use this method still and, as the pictures show, they generally sit on a stool or bench. In really early days, a spinner sat on the floor, with one leg doubled under him. He rolled the spindle down his other leg until it hit the floor, where it went on spinning. Then he brought it back in the way already described. Navaho women, who learned their spinning from the pueblos, use this old position still. But, say pueblo weavers, you would never mistake their thread for the thread spun by a Hopi man. They spin backward! This means that, instead of starting the spindle rolling away from them, from thigh to knee, they start it toward them, from knee to thigh.

Plate III-4. Hopi spinner, rolling the spindle on his thigh

Plate III-5. Pueblo spinner with spindle tip in pottery bowl

Plate III-6. A Hopi spinner evening the twist in his yarn

The result is a thread with a left-handed twist. Hopi thread, on the contrary, has a right-handed twist, like that of white man's string.

The Navaho use other spinning methods, also, and so do some of the eastern Pueblos, though Hopi and Zuni keep to the old fashioned "leg rolling" just described. One of these variations is to place the spindle tip on the floor, as in III-5. This is a method used by many Mexican and Peruvian Indians. Perhaps it came into use after the spindle was invented, for, as can be seen, the spindle is a necessary part of it. Leg rolling, on the other hand, could be done with the fingers, without any spindle at all.

The spinner in the sketch III-5 has made a further improvement common in the eastern pueblos. He has rested his spindle tip, not on the floor but in a small pottery bowl. That keeps it in position while it spins. The upper end of the spindle rests against his right leg. When he starts spinning, he pushes this upper end gently away from him. The spindle revolves as it moves and its lower tip moves forward along the floor or round and round in the bowl. The upper tip moves along his leg, then away, so that the spindle stands free, held in a slanting position by the fingers of his right hand and the pull on the yarn. When it has stopped spinning he brings it back and starts it again. In this case, too, there is a right-handed twist whereas the Navaho woman would start the spindle toward her and make a left-handed one.

All these directions apply also to second or third spinning and to the re-spinning of commercial yarn, which is never twisted tight enough for fine belts and blankets. Pueblos and Navaho unravelled red cloth or bayeta to get red yarn but they always had to spin it again before using it. The Hopi spun it again in the same direction, the Navaho in the opposite direction. It would be interesting to know what the other pueblos did and Indian students have an interesting subject for study here. Did the use of bayeta cause a change from left-handed to right-handed twist?

Pueblo yarn, even when finished, was often rough and knobby. It was smoothed by passing it over a corncob, like the one in III-3 **f.** Or, it might be drawn over a block of smooth sandstone. The ruins show many such blocks, grooved where the string has been drawn back and forth. Finally, the weaver sometimes singed it to remove loose ends.

Preparation of Wool.   Wool, when the pueblo finally got it, was spun just like cotton. It is hard to find out, at this late date, how they sheared and cleaned it. They certainly hacked it off the sheep without much system, using any sharp pieces of metal they could get from the Spaniards. Nor do we know how they carded it. Carding means pulling the curly wool fibres so that they all lie in one direction. There is some tradition that the pueblos combed them out with thistles, but since they can remember they have used white man's cards. These are flat pieces of wood, a little larger than the palm of the hand, with a handle on one flat side and the other side studded with steel points like a wire brush. The worker holds one card in each hand, with a pad of wool between them, and moves the cards across one another and away in opposite directions, drawing out the fibres. Ultimately these lie lengthwise in a fluffy hank. The process might be hard if the wool were curly but the hardy Merino sheep which the Spaniards gave the pueblos had long wool, loosely curled. Hand carding was enough and the wool had so little grease that it could even be handled for weaving without washing. Whether the sheep made good mutton was another matter.

The Navaho, who had so little water, often did not wash their wool. The pueblos say that they always did. They waited until after the carding was over, picking out burrs and dirt during the carding process. Then they soaked the wool over night in a jar of water or in a stream if this were the wet season. Next day they washed it in cold water and yucca root. If they wanted really white yarn, they boiled it a little. Then they bleached and dried it in the sun. Yarn from this type of wool could be washed after spinning if that was more convenient.

Dyeing Yarn. After spinning came dyeing. It is hard to tell now how frequently pueblo people colored their yarn and in what shades. Ancient belts and pack straps sometimes show a staining with earth colors—rusty red from haematite, yellow and orange from yellow ochre, turquoise blue from copper sulphate. When cotton came in, the weavers added some vegetable dyes—black, dark brown, and light blue. Women did the dyeing. They made large special pots for the purpose and kept these always clean and untouched by grease. Some recipes, remembered now, mention boiling the dye but there were ceremonial articles for which boiling was not proper. Recipes also mention alunogen, the native alum which can be found in small scattered deposits in the desert. Both pueblos and Navaho use it today to fix dye.

Occasionally, finished fabric was dyed by a method now forgotten in the pueblos but popular among whites. This is tie-dyeing. It meant that knots were tied in the cloth before it was placed in the dye bath. The cloth concealed inside these knots retained its former color, while the rest was dyed. Occasionally, also, cloth was painted in various patterns.

Pueblo people do little yarn dyeing at present though the Navaho, who seem to have learned weaving from them, do a great deal. It is hard to tell how many of the recipes now used by the Navaho were learned from pueblo teachers and how many were worked out by themselves. A few, remembered by old Zuni women or Hopi men about fifty years ago, are given below. Indian students might make an interesting project of looking up others.

Pueblo native dyes:

Black:	Sumac (rhus trilobata) boiled for an hour and a half with clay containing sulphate of iron, aluminum, and magnesium. (Navaho boil it with yellow ochre and pinyon gum)	Zu
	Black seeded sunflower, combined with pinyon gum and ochre	H
Blue:	Purplish blue, black seeded sunflower, as above.	H
	Dark blue, dark navy bean (cultivated).	
	Light blue, larkspur (Delphinium)	
	All blues, indigo (Indigofera Anil I tintoria) dissolved in children's urine. Shades could be made darker by boiling with black.	All pueblos

31

Red:	Brownish red, a grass (Thelesperma gracile).	H
	A more elaborate method remembered at Zuni was to soak the yarn for three days in alunogen and native lime (carbonat of calcium). It was removed and washed in yucca suds then boiled with an unidentified plant called mothlana, the vessel being emptied three times and refilled with fresh dye. Finally more alunogen was put in with blossoms of coreopsis (Coreopsis cardaminefolia). This combination also was emptied out three times and the vessel freshly filled.	Zu
	Pinkish red, purple corn (zea mais).	H
	Pink, pigweed (Amaranthus retroflexus).	H
	Bright red, made by unravelling scarlet cloth.	All pueblos
Yellow:	Rabbit brush flowers (Chrysothamnus bigelovi, Philostrophe tagelina).	H
Green:	Made by dyeing yarn yellow by either of the above methods then placing it for a short time in cold blue water. The Hopi got a yellowish green with rabbit brush only.	Zu
White:	Mix a sandy clay containing gypsum with warm water (not hot).	Zu

H—Hopi   Zu—Zuni

The Loom

Pueblo looms were not all of one type as many people suppose. Instead, there were two distinct types learned or worked out, perhaps, from different sources. One was the waist loom, used by weaving peoples all the way from Peru to the pueblos. The other, which came a little later, was the famous blanket loom of the Southwest, used by Hopi and Navaho today. There were a number of variations between, as there are still.

What Is a Loom?   A loom must do two things. First, it must hold the foundation strands, the warp, tight. This requires two parallel bars and usually they are adjustable so the threads can be tightened or loosened. The bar nearest the weaver, where the cloth is begun, is called the cloth beam. That furthest away, covered with yarn not yet woven, is the yarn beam.

Second, the loom must provide some arrangement for separating groups of warps by wholesale means, so the weft can be passed through quickly. Otherwise, the weaver would be endlessly at work, picking up one warp after another with his fingers. The device for separating warps is called a **heddle** (sometimes, heald).

Weavers, when classifying a loom, do not think first of whether it is wide or narrow, upright or lying flat. The point is how the warps are laid on and what is the heddle arrangement. Are the warps tied to a stick or passed through reeds or fastened to a lever? These are all different heddle arrangements and the passageway which they open between the warps is called a **shed.** Another way to put the question would be: How is the shed opened? With these facts in mind, we can go on to a description of the loom.

The Waist Loom. Probably one of the oldest forms of loom in the world is the frameless type shown in the photograph (III-10) and usually called the waist loom. Here the cloth beam and yarn beam are not set rigid in a frame but put in place each time the weaver begins to work. The yarn beam is attached to a tree, peg or, in our photograph, to the wall. The cloth beam is fastened, somehow, to the weaver's waist. The loom can be seen in many parts of the Old World even today and it was apparently invented again in the New. It was the standard loom in Peru, Guatemala, and Mexico, where the weavers were usually women. Somehow it came to the pueblos many centuries before the development of the big blanket loom with its fixed frame. Perhaps it brought with it the tradition of women weavers. At least many Pueblo women used the waist loom and do still. However, men used it also. At Hopi, men took over the weaving art altogether but it is interesting to see that they never fixed bars to their waist. Generally, they fastened them between floor and ceiling.

Warp Stringing for the Waist or Frameless Loom. Many weavers had permanent fixtures in their homes for warp winding and the diagrams (III-7, III-8) show these in a modern Hopi house.

First, two bars A and B are placed in position parallel with the floor and a little above it. One end of each is held in a hole in the wall (J and K). The other end of each bar lies against a heavy plank, I, where it is held in place by a circle of nails. The plank, in turn, is kept firm by a stone wedged against it. In the early days, when planks and nails were not to be had, the weaver kept on hand two heavy stone blocks, with holes pierced in their sides to receive the bars.

The Hopi weaver sits at X, holding in his hand the tight-spun cotton string, many yards long, which will form his warp. He ties one end of it to A, on the wall side then winds it over B under A, over B under A, like a towel on two rollers. This has been called a tubular form of warp, which seems a good name, since the diagram shows that the strings pass back and forth without intersecting and do, actually, form a wide flat tube. It is the best arrangement for long articles like belts which are woven in one continuous band. When cut apart, the band is twice the length of the loom, so that a belt nine feet long need have a cloth beam and yarn beam only four and a half feet apart. For blankets, the warp is strung differently.

The weaver keeps winding his warp back and forth until it forms a series of parallel threads as wide as the finished fabric is to be. This cannot

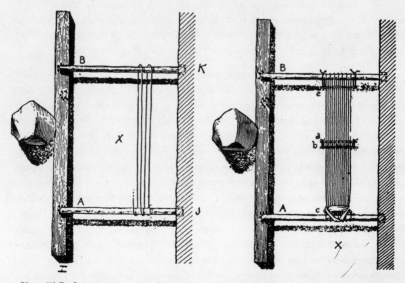

Plate III-7. Stringing the warp for waist loom

Plate III-8. Warp for waist loom, with heddles in place

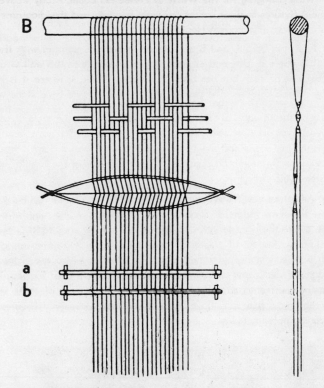

B

a
b

Plate III-9. Warp prepared for waist loom

be too wide if one bar of the loom is to be tied to his waist. Ancient fabrics from the pueblos or from Middle America are only about two feet wide and modern belts three or four inches.

The Stick Heddle.   The winding finished, the weaver fixes the final end of her string to one of the bars and then puts in the heddles. These are of the same type for almost all pueblo looms. Made of the simplest materials —smooth, slender sticks and long cotton string, they nevertheless take up little space and permit surprisingly fine weaving.

The sheds are "picked" only in the upper surface of the flat, tubular warp. The lower surface hangs straight, as shown in the profile sketch (right above) where the lower surface is at right, upper at left. To make the first shed, the weaver simply raises every alternate warp with his fingers and runs a slender rod through the opening thus made. This is the shed rod, **a** in the larger sketch above. It opens one shed and, to put a weft through, the weaver need only lay his thread alongside this rod. The second shed must raise the strands being held down by **a.** This is accomplished by tying those strands to .

35

the heddle stick **b,** which can be pulled forward, opening a different passage. The weaver picks up the warps left down before, and ties each to **b** with a continuous string. This passes over warp and stick, is fastened with a half hitch, then passes over the next warp and the stick. If the work is done, the warps lie evenly spaced and all held at the same tension.

The weaver now dismantles his warp stringing device, rolls up the warp and puts it away. The large sketch III-9 shows how he has guarded against tangling of the threads. Short sticks have been tied to the ends of shed rod and heddle rod so they will not fall out. Flexible sticks have been thrust through the two sheds and their ends tied together. Above them, three sticks have been run through both upper and lower surfaces of the tubular warp, to keep them lying straight.

Adjusting the Waist Loom. When the weaver sets up his loom he may use the same rollers, if they are not too heavy. Or, he may have a special set, cut to the right length and with knobs on the ends to keep the warp from slipping. Rollers of this sort have been found in the ruins, polished smooth with sandstone by some painstaking weaver. Also the diggers find pierced stone blocks and holes in the wall such as were used for warp stringing. In the fourteenth and fifteenth centuries, when most of these seem to have been made, they may have been as desirable household fixtures as an inset ironing board is today.

Plate III-10. Pueblo weaver with waist loom and reed heddle

36

Old houses also show stakes in the floor or pegs in the wall which may have served for attaching the further end of a waist loom. The near end, or cloth beam, is held to the waist in various ways. Perhaps there is attached to it a wide loop made of yucca rope, modern rope, or cloth. The weaver crawls inside this and sits leaning back against it, holding the warp stretched. Some pueblo women have a wide leather strap, fastened to the roller at one end and with a slit in the other, like a buttonhole. When working, the weaver sits on the floor and buttons the strap around her. When she gets up, she unbuttons the strap and lets cloth and warp fall to the floor.

The Reed Heddle. The photograph (III-10) shows a pueblo waist-loom weaver, posing at Washington in the early twentieth century. She uses a heddle common among Zuni and Hopi at that time and made of tiny uprights, set between parallel bars, some thirty inches long. These uprights are made of smooth, slender reeds but you can see the same thing, made of wire, in any little hand loom used by modern white women for weaving scarves and table linen. Each upright is pierced with a hole, like a needle with an eye in the center. The warp used with this heddle is not tubular, but made of separate strands, twelve feet long or more. When it is strung, the threads are passed alternately through the eye of an upright and through the space between two uprights. Half the threads, therefore, are held firm and half can slide up and down between the uprights. The weaver in the pueblo photograph has lowered her heddle, pushing down the threaded warps which appear across its center. The others have slid up to its top bar, thus opening a shed.

This is an old European form of heddle. For centuries, it was made of reeds by the peasants of Spain and France. When the power loom was developed, this same form of heddle was taken over and, even though it was made of steel, it was known as the "reed." Commercial weavers use that term still. We can guess that the Spaniards brought reed heddles to America, for Spanish-Americans are using them today in pueblo country. The alert pueblo weavers may have decided to copy them, for toward the end of the last century they were making clumsy heddles of mesquite sticks, tied together with leather thongs. Rarely could they get smooth reeds and milled lumber like those shown in the photograph. Evidently, they found the white man's device less efficient than their own stick heddles, whose loops of string took up so little room. There are no reed heddles in use today.

Other Forms of Tubular Loom. Almost as late as 1920, Isleta, San Felipe, and perhaps some other pueblos were still weaving belts on the waist loom. Still, many weavers must have thought of detaching the cloth bar from their waists and holding the warp firm in some other way. Hopi men fastened the cloth beam to the floor and yarn beam to the ceiling, just as they did later with the large blanket loom. (Plate III-11) Fixtures were built into the house for this purpose, and generally these took the form of a plank set into the stone floor. Holes were bored in the planks and leather loops passed through the holes, ready to receive a loom bar or the cord attached to it.

It can be seen that, when we once have the principle of the two rollers and the tubular warp, all sorts of arrangements are possible. Navaho women attach the two rollers between the prongs of a long, forked stick, so they can carry the whole contrivance around. Pupils at the Indian schools have, for a

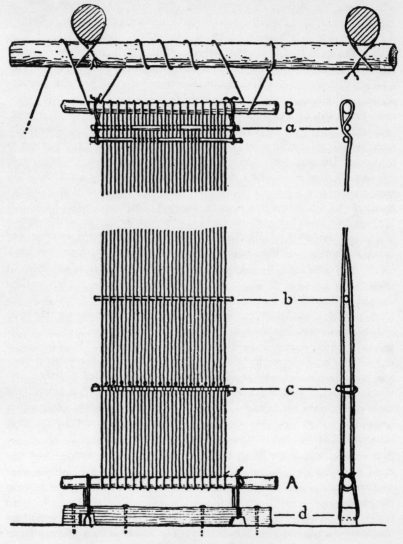

Plate III-11. Upright tubular loom

38

long time, used a rectangular frame of four pieces of wood and it is interesting that they and older people like to sit with it in their laps in the very position they would use with a waist loom. Often these frames have an extra stick to help keep the warp straight. This is put in when the warp is strung. Each thread, after passing over bar A and before passing over bar B, is looped once around the stick. The stick holds the strands in order but it can be pulled around the warp as it is moved.

This arrangement for pulling the warp around is one of the distinguishing things about any kind of tubular loom. It means that the warp can be pulled along on its rollers just as a roller towel is pulled, furnishing a fresh section of towel for each new person. In the same way the weaver on a tubular loom, when he or she has woven the nearby section, pulls the warp along and brings an unwoven section into place. This is not possible with the reed heddle, nor with the blanket loom, which is next to be described.

The Blanket Loom.   The tubular loom is suited to long, narrow fabrics. Peruvian weavers, when they wanted wider cloth, used to sew several strips together. Sometimes, one student has guessed, they even set several waist-loom weavers side by side, having them interlock the edges of their webs as they worked. The pueblos, somehow, developed a wide loom. No one knows how this came about but scraps in the ruins suggest that it happened between 1100 and 1300 A.D. Perhaps those old looms, whose poles and string have long since rotted, were like the blanket loom of today. This is the famous loom of the Southwest, thought of by many people as the only one. It is still used by Hopi and Navaho and once by many other pueblos.

The photograph (III-12) shows such a loom outside a Hopi house with a weaver of the 1890's sitting before it. This weaver is a man, as all Hopi weavers are except the weavers of a few women's belts. However, men seem to have used the blanket loom in many pueblos, in contrast to women, who used the waist loom. Of course the rule is not a fixed one. The Navaho, who learned weaving from the pueblos, leave it all to women, blanket loom and waist loom alike. From this we imagine that, even for the blanket loom, they may have had women teachers.

However, there is a difference of tradition connected with the narrow loom and the wide. The waist loom, throughout Peru and Middle America, is woman's work and perhaps the Southwest learned about it in that form. On the other hand, the wide frame for twining rabbitskin blankets was often used by men, the skinworkers. Old Paiute and Papago men, in Nevada and Arizona, remember the custom yet. Perhaps pueblo men also did such weaving, and when the blanket loom was somehow developed they considered it suitable for men's work.

The diagram (III-13) shows how this loom was rigged.   **a** and **b** are the already familiar bars which hold the warp.   **a** instead of being fastened to

39

Plate III-12. Hopi blanket loom

more tension in the fabric. From **c** hangs the upper loom bar. Looking at the photograph, you can see the same arrangement.

So far, we might be speaking of the tubular loom. However, though this does not show in the diagram, the warp **j** is not in tubular form. The finished fabric, therefore, will not be twice the length of the loom but, with a blanket, this is not necessary. In fact, the new situation has brought about a very clever arrangement. The warps are **crossed** while being strung, so that when the loom is set up, one shed is already in place. The weaver who first saw this possibility ranks as a real inventor, though we do not know when and where he worked. Second, the warps are not passed directly over bars **a** and **b** but over strings attached to these bars. These "loom strings" are **g** in the diagram. The warp is **j**. At each side of it are two heavily twisted strings, **k,** which will form the selvage of the blanket.

Warp Stringing for the Blanket Loom.   For particulars as to warp arrangement, we turn to the more detailed diagrams, (III-14). For stringing this warp, bars are set in place just as for stringing the waist loom and, in

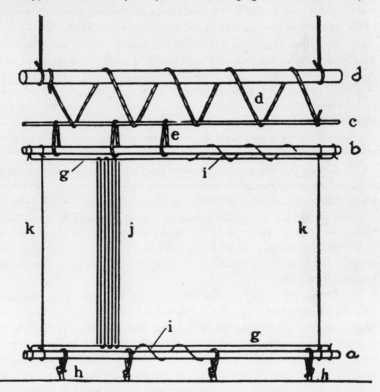

Plate III-13. Warp stringing for blanket loom

41

fact, the same bars may be used. The number of holes in the wall allows for their being set any distance apart. Warp is wound over these bars, not in the tubular form, over A over B but over A under B, forming a figure 8, as in Figs. 1 and 2 (III-14). Now the weaver inserts the loom strings, which will take the place of A and B when the warp is held upright in the loom. Fig. 3. Why strings instead of rods? Because the finished product is not to be a sash with fringe but a blanket with strong edge. The cords will form its upper and lower edges but meantime they have to bear the pull of the stretched warp so they must be strong. Each cord is made of specially spun string, or perhaps of two strings twisted. And then it is doubled. Its two parts twine through the warp, one over and one under, in the manner of the old fur blanket. If the warp is a fine one, with strings close together, this weft is twisted once between each two strings. If the warp is coarse it is twisted two or three times. Now the warp threads are held firm and evenly spaced.

Next, the loom strings must be stretched taut, so the warp will hang properly. The weaver takes the light rods, A and B in the diagram, and loops them to other rods, H and I. The cord loops over the rod, through the twining of the loom string, over the rod again, as in Figs. 4 and 5 (III-14).

Next the heddles are put on. If this were a tubular warp the weaver would have to open the first shed with his fingers and run a stick through it. As it is, the figure eight arrangement has already opened a shed. He runs a long stick through this, then picks up the alternate threads and attaches a stick to them. This is the heddle. If this is an elaborate weave, he may put in more heddles. He ties the ends of all heddles together so that they will not slip out, then takes the warp off the frame and perhaps puts it away. He may set it up for weaving in some other house or, if he is a Hopi, in the kiva.

Setting the Warp.   Old houses and kivas too had permanent fixtures for warp attachment. We have noted the heavy beam hung from the ceiling in diagram III-13 and outside the house in photograph III-12. For the floor end of the warp, there might be stakes as in diagram III-13 **h** or a beam attached to the floor, as in III-11 or 12. Sometimes the lower bar was held by leather loops put through grooves in a stone floor or a log sunk in an earthen floor. Old housebuilders provided for weaving fixtures as modern builders provided for wiring.

The bars in place, the warp is tightened. Now comes the last operation, the placing of selvage cords at the two sides (K in diagram III-13). Zuni people run three cords along beside the warp at each side, tying them to bars A and B instead of to the loom string. As each weft came to the edge of the warp, it passed over one of these and under the other two, always in alternate succession. Jemez people use one cord made up of two or three smaller ones, tightly twisted, and each weft passes between the cords of the twist at a different place. The twist becomes loosened in the operation and often has to

42

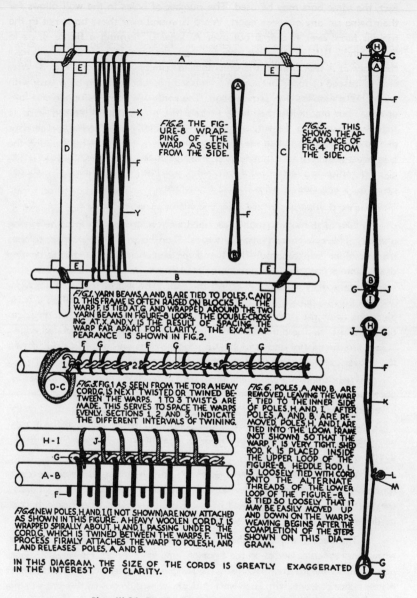

FIG.2. THE FIGURE-8 WRAPPING OF THE WARP AS SEEN FROM THE SIDE.

FIG.5. THIS SHOWS THE APPEARANCE OF FIG.4 FROM THE SIDE.

FIG.1. YARN BEAMS, A AND B, ARE TIED TO POLES, C, AND D. THIS FRAME IS OFTEN RAISED ON BLOCKS, E. THE WARP, F, IS TIED AT G, AND WRAPPED AROUND THE TWO YARN BEAMS IN FIGURE-8 LOOPS. THE DOUBLE-CROSSING AT X, AND Y, IS THE RESULT OF SPACING THE WARP FAR APART FOR CLARITY. THE EXACT APPEARANCE IS SHOWN IN FIG.2.

FIG.3. FIG.1 AS SEEN FROM THE TOP. A HEAVY CORD, G, IS NEXT TWISTED OR TWINED BETWEEN THE WARPS. 1 TO 3 TWISTS ARE MADE. THIS SERVES TO SPACE THE WARPS EVENLY. SECTIONS 1, 2, AND 3, INDICATE THE DIFFERENT INTERVALS OF TWINING.

FIG.6. POLES A, AND B, ARE REMOVED, LEAVING THE WARP F, TIED TO THE INNER SIDE OF POLES, H, AND, I. AFTER POLES, A, AND, B, ARE REMOVED, POLES, H, AND I, ARE TIED INTO THE LOOM FRAME (NOT SHOWN) SO THAT THE WARP, F, IS VERY TIGHT. SHED ROD, K, IS PLACED INSIDE THE UPPER LOOP OF THE FIGURE-8. HEDDLE ROD, L, IS LOOSELY TIED WITH CORD ONTO THE ALTERNATE THREADS OF THE LOWER LOOP OF THE FIGURE-8. L IS TIED SO LOOSELY THAT IT MAY BE EASILY MOVED UP AND DOWN ON THE WARPS. WEAVING BEGINS AFTER THE COMPLETION OF THE STEPS SHOWN ON THIS DIAGRAM.

FIG.4. NEW POLES, H, AND, I, (I NOT SHOWN) ARE NOW ATTACHED AS SHOWN IN THIS FIGURE. A HEAVY WOOLEN CORD, J, IS WRAPPED SPIRALLY ABOUT, H, AND, I, PASSING UNDER THE CORD, G, WHICH IS TWINED BETWEEN THE WARPS, F. THIS PROCESS FIRMLY ATTACHES THE WARP TO POLES, H, AND, I, AND RELEASES POLES, A, AND, B.

IN THIS DIAGRAM, THE SIZE OF THE CORDS IS GREATLY EXAGGERATED IN THE INTEREST OF CLARITY.

Plate III-14. Details of warp stringing for blanket loom

be untied and twisted again. There must have been other forms of selvage strings but they all insured a strong edge at the side of the fabric, as the loom strings insured it at top and bottom.

In any case, stringing and setting up the warp was a day's work. Hopi men preparing to weave the square white blanket for bride set the date days ahead so that a group could gather. They worked all day in the kiva and expected a feast of mutton stew from the bride's relatives at the day's end.

Weaving Tools. The weaver has his own tools, made of hard, fine grained wood and polished smooth, so they will not catch on the threads. The first is the batten, a slender, swordlike piece of wood which varies in length and width according to the work. It may be merely a flattened rod, like **a** or **b** in photograph III-3. It may have a wider surface and sharpened edge, like **c,** a type which is often called the weaving sword. It may be carved to a shape like a butcher's cleaver, with handle and blade.

The batten is an all-purpose tool. When the weaver has opened a shed, in any of the ways already described, he runs the batten in as he would a knife, holding it flat against the warps. Then he turns it crosswise, as the man has done in photograph III-31 and the woman in III-10. This holds the shed open so that the weft can pass through easily. In pueblo and Navaho weaving no tool is used for inserting the weft. The weaver pokes it through with his fingers, holding it in a ball or wound on a slender stick. When it is in place, he turns the batten flat against the warps again and pushes its edge down against the thread. Here is the reason for the slightly sharpened edge. It lays the thread flat and straight, tight against the one below it. This done, the weaver opens another shed and inserts the batten again.

He has one other tool, the fork, seen in the left hand of the weaver in photograph III-12. It is a trowel-shaped piece of wood, with teeth cut in its lower edge. After two or three rows of weft have been put in and pushed down with the batten, the weaver inserts the teeth of the fork between the warps and presses again, more thoroughly—or in some cases, beats the threads down.

Weaving Methods. Most garments had an oblong shape and, except for blankets, they were woven so that the warp ran the short way of the goods, the weft the long way. This was because, so often, the longer side had a border which must be specially woven.

The weaver started at the lower edge of the fabric which was the one within easy reach as he sat on the floor or some low support. He wove straight across which meant that if he was making a wide blanket he must move his seat once or twice, with each weft. Navajo women do not do this but sit still and put in the wefts part way across and as far up as they can reach. Their finished blankets show faint diagonal lines where the joints have been made, and the Hopi call these "lazy lines." They are a good means of telling a Navaho blanket from one made in pueblos, but are not infallible. A few pueblo weavers admit that they, too, leave "lazy lines" now and then.

There were other differences from the Navajo, too, which may be interesting to notice. As a weaver puts in his wefts one above the other, he is very likely to draw the warp strands in a little, so that the blanket looks tied in at the waist. Navajo weavers have spoken of this trouble but they do not use a mechanical device to prevent it. Pueblos often tie a bar to the back of the warp to hold it out exactly as wide as it should be.

Navaho weavers when they get about to the middle of a blanket lower the bar D so that the section where they are working is brought down closer. This leaves a loop of finished material which they double under the lower bar, A and sew there. Then they weave straight on to the top. The last threads of weft, just under the loom string, are hard to put in and the weaver uses a narrower batten. Finally she gives up battens entirely and picks the warps apart with her fingers. The very last threads must be put through with a darning needle. Even so, they are looser and more irregular than other wefts. This would not matter in a Navaho blanket for the top stripe would simply seem wider, as it often does.

With pueblo fabrics this would not do. The fabric often had a border at top and bottom made in different weave than the main part, and the borders must be identical. Sometimes the borders were to be embroidered, which meant counting threads. That would lead to tragedy if there were not always the same number to the inch. Not that pueblo people counted in inches but they knew how to make the number of threads come out right. Their arrangement for getting equal tension at both borders was to weave to the middle of a fabric, then detach bars A and B and turn the warp upside down, with A at the top and B at the bottom. The weaver in photograph III-12 has done this and you can see a finished border at the top of his fabric, while he is working on another at the bottom. The result is that the loose, difficult stitches come in the middle of the fabric instead of at one end. This "soft part" can generally be seen if you hold a pueblo kilt or manta up to the light.

Weaves

The type of loom does not determine the type of fabric. It is true that the waist loom is more convenient for narrow goods and the blanket loom for broad ones, but subject to limitations of width any weave could be used on any of them. The thing which decides weave is not how the shed is opened but **which threads compose the shed.** If several selections of threads are made, this means several heddles, differently attached. (See page 43 for further explanation of "heddles.")

The pueblos must have experimented a good deal with heddles and often they changed the weave when they were part way through a garment. One who looks for the first time at a woman's blanket dress, for instance, might not realize that it has two distinct weaves, and neither of them simple. The same is true of kilts and shawls and breechcloths. Even when they are in plain color, they may have an elaborate weave.

Plain Weave.　　The plain weave has the minimum of sheds—two. They are controlled by two heddles or a heddle and a shed stick, raising alternate warps, so that the weft crosses over one under one. A burlap sack shows a coarse version of this.

Plain Weave—Basket.　　When the warp and wefts are of equal thickness and combined loosely enough so that both of them show in the finished product, the weave looks like a basket. (III-15) This is a frequent pattern with cotton materials, since cotton is not elastic and it would be hard to crowd or stretch either warp or weft so as to hide the other. That was one reason for the frequent use of such a weave in the pueblos. The other was that the evenly spaced threads, which resemble those of coarse canvas, made the best basis for embroidery. The threads, as counted by modern embroiderers, are 24 to the inch.

Articles Made in Basket Weave

Woman's large white cotton shawl, the Hopi "wedding robe." (See Plate III-16)

White shawls of any size to be embroidered.

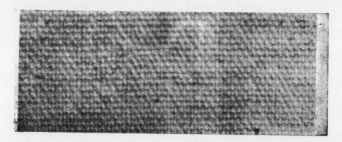

Plate III-15. Close-up of plain weave

46

Plate III-16. Hopi wedding shawl in basket weave

Borders of woman's woolen blanket dress if to be embroidered.

Man's white cotton kilt.

Man's shirt (wool or cotton) if to be embroidered. (Plate III-41)

Plain portion of man's patterned sash.

Whole white sash done by some pueblos in imitation of the Hopi braid-ed sash.

Small woolen blankets for boys and babies.

Plain Weave—Blanket. The plain weave is sometimes spoken of as blanket if the weft is heavier than the warp and so crowded together that

47

the warp does not show. This is a good weave with wool, where the weft may be soft and fluffy and the warp fine-spun and tight. It is a usual one with Navaho and pueblo blankets, where the colored weft carries the whole pattern and the warp is invisible. The warp may even be of cotton thread or string.

Articles Made in Blanket Weave

Woolen blankets, for bedding and men's wear, usually were white with plain stripes of blue, brown, or black running the short way of the blanket. Zuni made them all black. Woolen blankets were once made by every pueblo except Tiwa. Now only Hopi and Santo Domingo make them in heavy rug form, for the tourist trade. (Plate III-17)

Twilled Weave. In twilled weaving the weft does not pass over every other warp, but over every two, every three, or even more, each weft crossing the warp at a point one thread to the right or left of the one below it. Plate III-20 shows how this produces a series of diagonal ribs across the fabric, instead of the vertical ribs of plain weaving. The same effect can be seen in modern serge, whipcord, and some tweeds. Tweed, in fact, is only another way of saying twill. We are familiar with the same pattern in basketry,

Plate III-17. Hopi striped woolen blanket

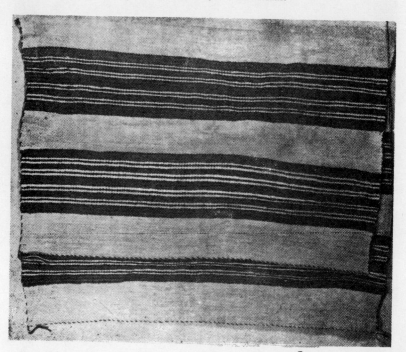

48

where the yucca tray (II-8) and the floor mat (II-7) were plaited (the basketry equivalent of weaving) in diagonal twill. Even yucca fibre sandals were twilled, for the method seems to have been a favorite with the Anasazi.

Some time before 1000 A.D. they had begun to make a twilled weave in cloth and the ruins of the famous Four Corners region abound in scraps of such material. The weavers had even gone on to variations such as the V shape and the diamond. All these are made with four sheds, as described below but the sheds pick up different warps and are used in different order.

Diagonal Twill. Plate III-18 shows the simplest form of diagonal twill, where the weft passes over two warps and under two. Looking at the warp numbers we can see that such a pattern cannot be made by opening only two sheds. There must be four, picking up the following warps.

Shed No. 1 warps 1, 2, 5, 6, 9, 10, 13, 14.
Shed No. 2 warps 2, 3, 6, 7, 10, 11.
Shed No. 3 warps 3, 4, 7, 8, 11, 12.
Shed No. 4 warps 1, 4, 5, 8, 9, 12, 13.

After this we go back to No. 1 again and open the sheds in regular order. This pattern is generally made on a blanket loom and the sheds are opened by one stick and three heddles. The arrangement can be seen in plate III-12 where the weaver is making the central, diagonal portion of a woman's blanket dress. His shed stick is visible near the top of the warp, with the three heddles below, one almost hidden behind the other two.

He might make the diagonal in various ways, passing the weft over three warps and under two, or over three under one; over three under three; over two under one.

Articles Made in Diagonal Twill

Woman's dark wool blanket dress, center section. The borders were usually in some other weave.

Woman's small white cotton shawl. This was the shawl which had a red and blue borders of which the red, too, was in diagonal weave. (See plate III-19)

Man's woolen shirts, kilts and breechcloths, usually in dark blue or black.

LEFT TWILL   1 2 3 4
RIGHT TWILL   1 4 3 2

Plate III-18. Diagram of twill weave

49

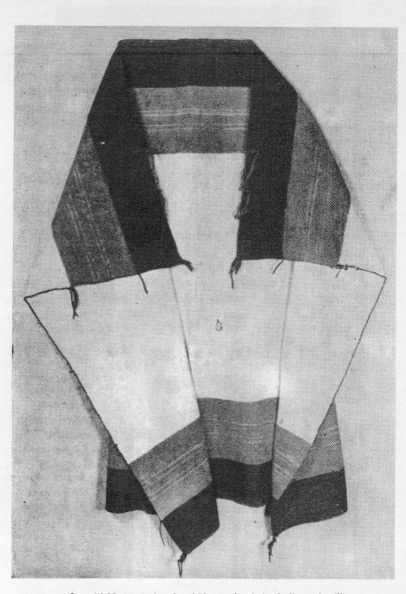

Plate III-19. Maiden's red and blue bordered shawl, diagonal twill

Plate III-20. Fabric in a diamond twill, small diamonds

Man's white ceremonial sash made in modern times, instead of the braided sash. (Plate III-36)

Herringbone or V-shaped Twill. The lines of diagonal twill can be broken and their direction changed, so that they form a series of V's. This pattern, very frequent in tweed, is called a herringbone. The pueblos used it in prehistoric days. Their herringbones were both horizontal and vertical.

Herringbone twill, therefore, is begun exactly like diagonal, with the heddles attached in the same way. A glance at diagram III-21 will show that the first four sheds are opened in the same order as they would be for diagonal. The change comes when the angle, or elbow of the herringbone is reached. Then the heddle order is reversed. Instead of 1234, 1234, it becomes 1234, 321, 234, 321.

Herringbone weave was used oftenest in combination with others. It can be seen in the Hopi boy's woolen blanket, in black and white plaid— Scotch plaid, we have called it. Here the warp and weft both are in wide strips of black and white. Throughout one or more weft strips the weave is herringbone, then the sheds are opened in different color, as described below, to produce diamond weave. (Plate III-23)

1   2   3   4   5   6   7   8   9   10   11   12   13   14

Plate III-21. Diagram of herringbone variation of twill weave

51

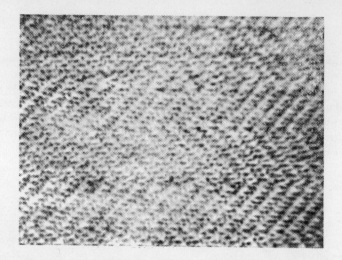

Plate III-22. Herringbone or V-shaped twill

Plate III-23. Hopi boy's blanket, the gray squares in herringbone

Diamond Weave. In diamond weave, there is a real change for here uneven numbers of warps must be picked up in order to produce diamond figures which are wide in the middle, narrow at both ends. Using diamonds of the same scale as the diagonal and herringbone already diagrammed, warps would be picked up as follows:

Shed No. 1 raises warps 1, 2, 4, 5, 8.
Shed No. 2 raises warps 1, 5, 6, 10.
Shed No. 3 raises warps 3, 6, 7, 9, 10.
Shed No. 4 raises warps 2, 3, 4, 7, 8, 9.

Any weaver can make a plan for diamonds large, small, many or few by drawing the design she wants in dots on checkered paper and numbering the warps. She can then see plainly the order in which her four sheds must be opened and the number of warp threads necessary for a diamond of the desired size.

Navaho rugs are sometimes made with as many as seven concentric diamonds, all in different colors. The pueblos use only one color and they

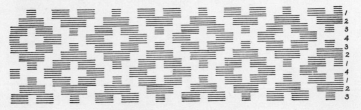

Plate III-24. Diagram of diamond weave

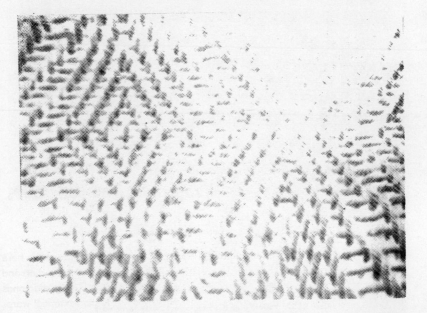

Plate III-25. Close-up of diamond twill weave

prefer two or three small diamonds although more are sometimes made. They use the diamond pattern generally as a border on garments made in some other weave. In that case the loom is rigged first for the diamond twill and one border woven. Then the warp is reversed and the other border woven. After this, the heddles have all to be untied and tied again differently. The weaver in plate III-12 seems to have woven both borders of a woman's blanket dress and to be now attacking the central portion.

Articles Made in Diamond Weave

Border of woman's dark woolen blanket dress when this was not to be embroidered. (Plate III-28)

Blue border of small white shawl. (Plate III-20)

Ends of man's woolen breechcloth.

Black and white plaid Hopi blanket. (Plate III-23)

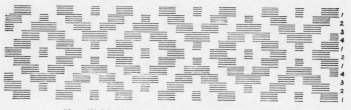

Plate III-26. Variation of diamond weave, twelve warp

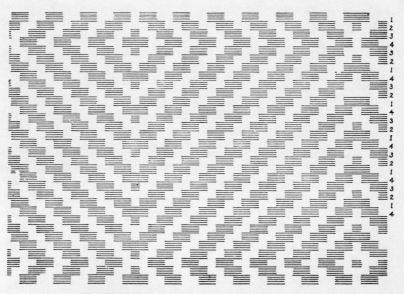

Plate III-27. Variation of diamond weave, sixty-three warp

54

Floated Warp (The Woman's Belt Pattern).   In the weaving of striped blankets, we noted that color is furnished entirely by the weft, while the warp does not show. In the woman's belt, the opposite is the case. Here, the pattern is made by warp threads of colored wool, while the weft which holds them together may be fine black or white thread which is almost invisible. This behind-the-scenes weft of cotton or linen may be called by the weavers' name, "tabby."

The colored warp, in these days, is always commercial yarn but it has to be re-spun to make it tight enough. The design is usually a border stripe of green or black down the whole length of the belt, then a vivid red background down the center, with a series of small designs in black or white. Each pueblo has its own favorite pattern while one popular design in red, green, and white is made by the pueblos to sell to the Navajo. Such belts must have been made long before the pueblos got commercial yarn or even wool, for fragments of them have been found in the ruins. Perhaps they were a common product of the old waist loom for Indian women of Middle America can still be seen wearing them and an ancient example has come from Peru.

This narrow fabric, nine feet long, is best woven in tubular form on the waist loom or on a narrow, upright loom. The weaver begins at one side and puts on the proper number of warp threads for the black or green border stripes, then ties on a red thread and begins with the background. He carries this across the whole space where the design is to be, but in the design area he spaces the threads a little further apart. Then he lays other warp threads of green or black over or between them so that, through the part where the design is to be, the warp is practically double. It is this double warp which will make it possible to "float" certain warp threads, that is, let

55

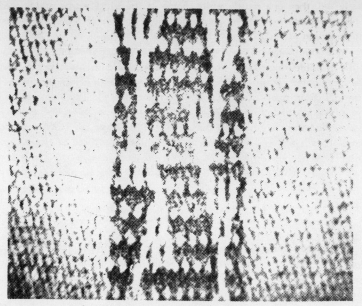

Plate III-29. Section of garter in floated warp weave

two or three wefts in succession pass under them so that they stand out to make a design. On the under side, threads of the opposite color will stand out. Threads for the border on the opposite side duplicate those for the first border and the whole warp has about 150 threads packed into six inches of width.

With his fingers the weaver picks out two sheds in the upper side of his tubular warp and adjusts a heddle and a shed stick as for plain weaving. In the central, doubled portion he has been careful to put all warps of the same color into the same shed.

He begins weaving at the end of the belt nearest him and alternates heddle and shed stick in the regular way, producing a green or black stripe where the warps are in those colors, red in the center. (See plate III-30) When he is ready for the first design he raises one heddle and applies the batten as usual, then, before going on to the next shed, he uses his fingers or a small stick to pick an extra small shed through the double warp. He passes the weft through and beats it down, pushing the unused warps to the under side of the fabric. This will bring out the design in warp threads which are raised or "floated" above the surface of the belt on both sides. The photograph III-29 shows a section of garter made in this way. The two borders are of white wool, in plain weave, the white warps being visible, while the linen "tabby" weft does not show. The center section has a double layer of red and white warps, picked up in such a way as to show first a row which is mostly red, then one mostly white. Some of the white warps are floated over two wefts and others over four, making a pattern of linked triangles. The same design will appear in red on the wrong side.

With this system of hand picking an extra shed, any number of variations are possible. Instead of having the background in plain weave and the design floated, as in the photograph, the background may be floated and the design in plain weave. Or both may be floated. The warps of the central patterned section may be of different thickness as in the popular red and white belt often made by pueblo people to sell to the Navaho. Here the warp threads of the background are red wool while those of the design are white cotton, like the weft tabby. Some weavers always pick the extra shed with their fingers, others use a slender stick. In the simpler cases, it is possible to adjust two small supplementary heddles across the patterned section.

As the weaver works, he (or she) pulls the warp around on its rollers, so that he always has an unworked section in front of him. He fastens his last weft, leaving two feet of the tubular warp unwoven. This is cut in two to form a fringe.

Articles Made in Floated Warp Weave

Woman's woolen belt. (Plate III-30)
Man's woolen garter. (Plate III-29)
Man's woolen headband.

Embroidery Weaving (sometimes called brocading). An unusual form of weaving, practiced only by the Hopi, is found in the brilliantly patterned ends of the man's ceremonial sash. (Plate III-34) At first sight, it looks like embroidery and, in fact, embroidery weaving seems the best name for it. Brocade, a name occasionally used, is condemned by professional weavers since the design does not show in reverse, on the wrong side, as in white man's brocade. We are faced here, as often in weaving descriptions,

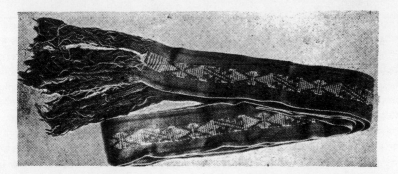

Plate III-30. Woman's belt in red and white, with design in floated warp

57

with the fact that the terms used for European weaves do not quite fit those of American Indians.

Embroidery weaving, for instance, is unlike anything made in Europe. More than that, it is unlike any fabric from Peru. This weave, in this case, seems to be an elaboration worked out by pueblo weavers and never achieved by the workers further south. Was it suggested by Spanish fabrics which pueblo people tried to imitate on their looms? There are no signs of it in the ruins of pre-Spanish days and all examples known are made with commercial yarn. That suggests a late origin but does not prove it, so we are left guessing.

The work at present is done by Hopi men, on the edges of white cotton sashes and kilts which are to be used in ceremonies. The main part of the garment is of white cotton in plain weave which shows at the bottom in plate III-34 and on the wrong side. At the border is a striking design in black and green wool, with touches of white. Looking at plate III-34, you see that the outstanding thing about this decoration is the heavy vertical ribs, which run through the pattern from top to bottom. A white weaver would produce such ribs by using an extra heavy warp. The Hopi weaver uses regular cotton warp but each of his colored weft strands, instead of merely passing under a warp at the proper point, is **wrapped once around,** causing such warps to stand out like ribs. This wrapping needs a special heddle arrangement.

The basis of it is a blanket loom on a small scale. Plate III-31 shows a Hopi weaver sitting at such a loom and plate III-32 shows the loom rig in detail. Though this loom may have only 150 warps as compared with the many hundreds on a blanket loom, the warps are crossed in the same way, not tubular. This, of course, will not allow the weaving of a six-foot sash all in one piece. It is made in two pieces which are sewed together through the plain white section. The weaver in the photograph has almost finished one such half of a sash.

Plates III-32, 33 show that this loom has a heddle **h** and a shed stick **j** as for plain weaving. Also, as in plain weaving, there are selvage strands **m** at each side, which are twisted, after each weft goes through, to make a strong edge. In the case of a sash, whose edges will have hard wear, there are four selvage strands at each side, instead of the usual two. So far, the loom looks like a blanket loom, shrunk to small scale. Its distinguishing feature is the extra heddle **g** which will produce the ribs. This heddle is so tied to the warps as to pull two forward and leave the next **eight** back all the way across the fabric. The weaver ties it on while rigging his loom but he will use it only for the patterned section. When this is finished, he will detach it, as the weaver in the photograph seems to have done for there only the regular heddle and shed stick are visible.

58

Plate III-31, Hopi man weaving a sash on an upright loom

59

The weaver begins work by putting in a few rows of white cotton weft, opening alternate sheds with heddle and shed stick in the usual way. When he is ready for the patterned section, he discards this cotton weft and uses, instead, the bright commercial wool which will do the wrapping and a thin linen tabby which will hold it in place. For the wrapping process, he pulls the extra heddle, thus bringing forward pairs of warps, at intervals of eight

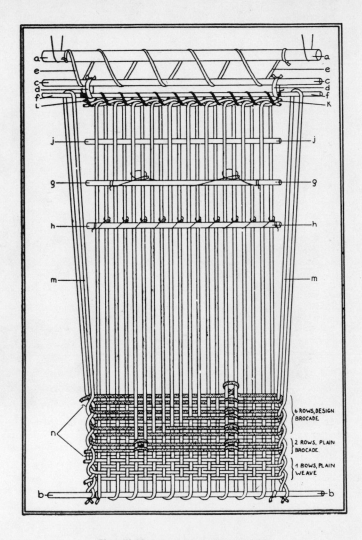

Plate III-32, Loom for embroidery weaving

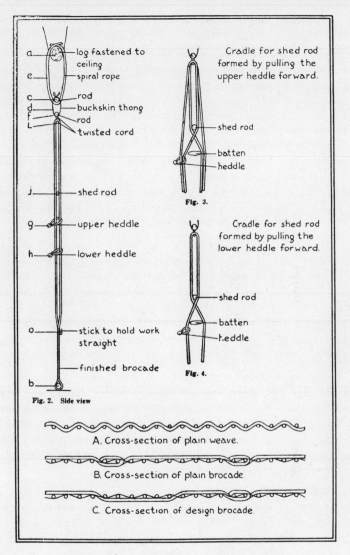

a — log fastened to ceiling
e — spiral rope
c — rod
d — buckskin thong
f — rod
L — twisted cord

j — shed rod

g — upper heddle

h — lower heddle

o — stick to hold work straight

— finished brocade

b —

Fig. 2. Side view

Cradle for shed rod formed by pulling the upper heddle forward.

— shed rod

— batten
— heddle

Fig. 3.

Cradle for shed rod formed by pulling the lower heddle forward.

— shed rod

— batten
— heddle

Fig. 4.

A. Cross-section of plain weave.

B. Cross-section of plain brocade.

C. Cross-section of design brocade.

Plate III-33. Position of heddles in embroidery weaving

warps apart, all the way across the fabric. He uses his fingers to wrap the bright wool weft once around the first pair of warps. Then he carries it along in front of the eight warps which the heddle leaves back, then once around the next pair brought forward and so on. At the edge where the four selvage strands are twisted tightly together, he passes the colored weft through this selvage rope, then leaves it hanging.

Next, he lifts the regular heddle and puts in a weft of invisible tabby; then the extra heddle again. It lifts the same pairs of warps as before and he passes the colored strand back in the opposite direction, again wrapping it once around each pair before he proceeds. Then he uses the shed stick for another row of plain tabby weft. It will be seen that all the actual weaving is done by the tabby and that, if the colored wool were omitted, we should have a plain fabric, though with very thin weft. The function of the colored wool is not weaving, for it wraps the same pairs of warps every time. If it were not for tabby, these warps with their connecting weft strands would hang out from the others in a loose mass. Actually, the function of the colored wool is only decoration, which may well be called embroidery weaving.

The small white figures seen in plate III-34 are another matter. Here, the process of passing the colored weft around a pair of warps, then in front of eight others, has been interrupted. Instead, the weaver has used his fingers to pass the bright yarn behind one or more warps, so that their white color is left showing. In the figures which look like a tall, thin C, we see the white warp with the marks of the thin tabby across it. In the large diamond figures, there are small white diamonds and triangles and, between them, a loose wool weft of some pale color, passing in front of several warps.

The weaver proceeds through the patterned section, using the heddle, extra heddle, shed stick, extra heddle and so on, occasionally bringing forward special warps to produce the white figures. When he has finished this section, he detaches the extra heddle, brings out his white cotton weft and finishes in plain weave. He weaves two identical pieces in this way and sews them together. At the patterned end of each, he has left a foot or so of unwoven warp, which serves as fringe.

The Braided Sash (also called rain sash and Hopi wedding sash). This broad, fringed white sash is made of warp only, with no weft at all. We shall speak of the process as braiding and it is, in fact, the same used in braiding women's hair except that here there are 150 strands to intertwine instead of three. Pueblo people must have known this technique in very early days for bits of braided fabric have been found in the ruins, dating earlier than other kinds of cloth. Indians of the Great Lakes knew the process also. Their narrow, bright-colored sashes of commercial wool were the regular wear for French trappers in colonial days and students have wondered whether the art was imported from Europe. Evidence shows, however, that the opposite was probably the case. Braiding was an Indian art, taught to French Canadians, who use it still. It may be, then, that this form of weftless

Plate III-34. Section of Hopi sash in embroidery weaves

63

weaving was known to many American Indian tribes, who never went beyond it to learn true weaving. (Plate III-36)

The Hopi practice it in elaborate form, making a sash over a foot wide, with a unique kind of fringe. For this purpose, they need something like a loom, to hold the strands in order and bring them across one another at regular intervals. What they use is a pair of rollers, arranged horizontally as for warp stringing. On these the worker winds his warp of two-ply white cotton in tubular form. Then, instead of picking sheds and attaching heddles, he starts crossing the strands over one another in regular order. The first at the left, and every sixth one after that, crosses under the next three to the right as in plate III-35, and then continues on down, while every sixth from the right crosses in the same way toward the left. Ultimately, every strand in the belt gets several turns at being sixth.

To hold this complicated interlocking in place, a smooth stick is run in after each. The diagram shows four such sticks in place. The worker, as he proceeds, puts in fifty of them, pulling the warp strands around on the rollers now and then, just as a belt weaver would do. As he braids on the upper side of the tubular warp, the strands on the lower side, their ends not free to disentangle as the ends of braided hair would be, twist themselves up in the opposite direction. Therefore he is actually braiding two sides of the warp at once. He stops long before the two sides meet, leaving a stretch of warp strings three or four feet long which is cut in two to serve as fringe at each end of the sash.

The fringe is a very important item and receives special treatment. The worker buries it in damp sand so it will twist more easily. Then he separates the strings into groups of six, ties each group at the end and rolls it on his leg into a twisted cord. (This, it happens, is a left-handed twist, not right.) He ties these twists together at the sash end, so that they hang in pairs and rubs them with white clay to whiten them.

A distinguishing mark to the Hopi sash, unknown to other Indian weavers, is the decorative knobs above the fringe. These are made of cornhusk rings covered with two-ply cotton string. The string is first wound over a short piece of wood, which has a length of string along each of its edges, just as a loom string runs along the loom bars except that, in this case, string and bar are not fastened together. The cotton is wound over wood and string in tubular form, then the wood is slipped out, the cotton covering is laid over the cornhusk ring and the two strings gather it into bag shape at top and bottom. (Plate III-39) One such ring is slipped over each pair of fringes. Plate III-37 shows the finished sash. Note the long vertical lines and the absence of horizontal ones such as are produced by weft threads.

True Embroidery. In present days, one of the striking things about pueblo ceremonial dress is the bright colored embroidery on kilts, sashes,

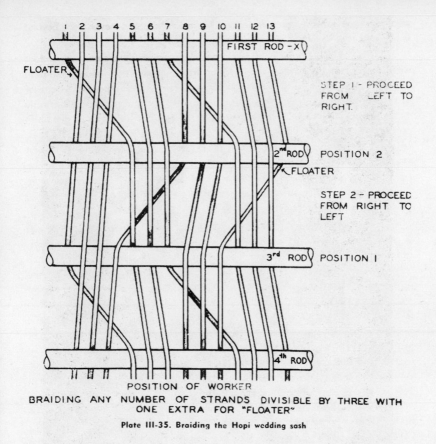

1 2 3 4 5 6 7 8 9 10 11 12 13

FIRST ROD - X

FLOATER

STEP 1 - PROCEED FROM LEFT TO RIGHT.

2nd ROD POSITION 2

FLOATER

STEP 2 - PROCEED FROM RIGHT TO LEFT

3rd ROD POSITION 1

4th ROD

POSITION OF WORKER

BRAIDING ANY NUMBER OF STRANDS DIVISIBLE BY THREE WITH ONE EXTRA FOR "FLOATER"

Plate III-35. Braiding the Hopi wedding sash

shawls and women's dresses. All of this is done with commercial wool and no known piece is over seventy years old. This means they were made after the pueblos became part of the United States and after the railroads

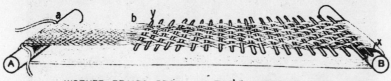

WORKER BRAIDS FROM "a" TO "b", INSERTING RODS AFTER EACH STEP, WHICH ARE PUSHED AWAY FROM WORKER TOWARD POLE B. "x" IS THE FIRST ROD INSERTED AND "y" IS THE LAST. NOTE BRAIDING IS DONE ENTIRELY ON UPPER PLANE.

Plate III-36. Braiding the Hopi sash

Plate III-37. The braided sash, with spindle, card, cotton, and beater

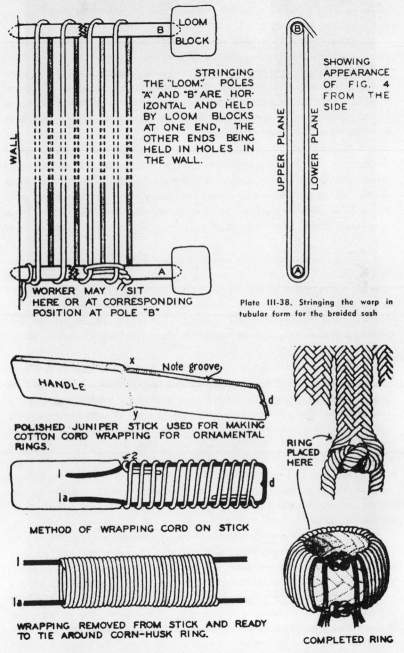

STRINGING
THE "LOOM". POLES
"A" AND "B" ARE HOR-
IZONTAL AND HELD
BY LOOM BLOCKS
AT ONE END, THE
OTHER ENDS BEING
HELD IN HOLES IN
THE WALL.

LOOM
BLOCK
B

WALL

WORKER MAY SIT
HERE OR AT CORRESPONDING
POSITION AT POLE "B"

A

SHOWING
APPEARANCE
OF FIG. 4
FROM THE
SIDE.

B

UPPER PLANE

LOWER PLANE

A

Plate III-38. Stringing the warp in tubular form for the braided sash

HANDLE

x   Note groove

y   d

POLISHED JUNIPER STICK USED FOR MAKING
COTTON CORD WRAPPING FOR ORNAMENTAL
RINGS.

l

la   d

METHOD OF WRAPPING CORD ON STICK

RING
PLACED
HERE

l

la

WRAPPING REMOVED FROM STICK AND READY
TO TIE AROUND CORN-HUSK RING.

COMPLETED RING

Plate III-39. Making the corn husk tassels for the braided sash

began to bring commercial wool. However, the stitch and the design belong distinctively to the pueblos.

The stitch is something like what white embroiderers call an outline stitch which means that it produces a solid line in which each new stitch slightly overlaps the one behind it. In pueblo embroidery, each stitch passes through the wool of the preceding stitch, thus splitting the stitch instead of lying beside it. This split stitch technique is an old one in coiled basketry so pueblo people, even if they learned embroidery from the whites, may have continued to use old sewing methods.

In the Plate III-40 the background of the pattern is composed of vertical rows done in this pueblo outline stitch. The white cloud symbol in the center is produced in the same way but the fine white zig-zag lines have another technique. Here the colored embroidery yarn has simply skipped a thread or two, leaving the plain white fabric showing. The result is that these lines look indented, while the rest of the pattern stands out from the cloth, in heavy wool.

Skipping threads in this way means very careful counting of stitches. This is, in fact, the essence of pueblo embroidery. The work was always done on native cotton cloth, in plain basket weave, and we have mentioned earlier that the weaving must be absolutely even so that the counting of stitches would produce the right spacing. In the present day, pueblo embroiderers sometimes use monk's cloth or coarse sacking which also are in basket weave.

They keep to a few colors: black, dark blue and dark green, with touches of red and yellow. These colors look very striking on the edge of a large white cotton shawl, like those draped around the masked figure of the Zuni Shalako. The same colors, without the yellow, are used on men's white sashes and kilts, which are often embroidered in these days, in imitation of the more difficult embroidery weaving which only the Hopi can do. The woman's blanket dress has often a deep row of embroidery along the lower edge. Zuni does this in dark blue, like the dress, while Acoma, Laguna and Tesuque like to introduce touches of red. In fact, pueblo people often recognize a garment embroidered at Acoma by the quantity of red which its women like to use.

Women are the embroiderers. At least, they are in all of the pueblos but Hopi. Hopi men, who do most of the weaving, have usurped the art of embroidery also, using the same designs as in their embroidery weaving. So do all who embroider sashes and kilts, for these have standard designs referring to fields and rainclouds. Some of the other designs look surprisingly like old ones found on basketry and pottery. For instance, the white zig-zag in Plate III-40, is one very familiar on coiled basketry. The sunflower, seen on Shalako robes, is an old standby on certain pots. Perhaps the women

Plate III-40. Detail of white embroidered robe

Plate III-41. Man's embroidered shirt (wool or cotton)

embroiderers, even though they use modern needles and wool, are keeping
to the patterns made familiar by their own ancient arts.

Articles Embroidered

Man's ceremonial kilt when not decorated by embroidery weaving
Man's patterned sash when not decorated by embroidery weaving
Man's shirt   (Plate III-41)
Man's breechcloth
Woman's large white shawl
Woman's blanket dress

Chapter IV

POTTERY STILL A LIVING ART

WOMEN made the pots, just as they did the baskets, and every woman made her own. This was the case everywhere, in early days, both in the old world and the new, for pots and baskets were women's tools, and the usual rule was that the person who was going to use a tool should make it. However, some six thousand years ago, the old world took the first step toward making pottery by machinery. This was the invention of the potter's wheel, a hand-twirled disc which shaped pots more quickly and evenly than they could be built up by hand. After this, pottery making became a trade, which could be carried on by one person for a whole village. Men took it up, and the housewives, instead of making their own kitchenware, traded for it with the potter. There are villages in Spain, today, which have gone no further in pottery manufacture than this hand-turned wheel.

The new world, however, never invented the wheel for wagons, machines, or even pottery. Each woman built up her jars slowly by hand, polished them, and finally baked them, turning the soft clay into hard earthenware. The women became skilled craftsmen and also artists, for they decorated their pottery wherever it was possible. In fact, most of our knowledge of the art of the ancient pueblos comes from designs painted by women on jars and bowls. These may be broken but they never crumble into earth and one of the chief tasks of the diggers is selecting the broken pieces of a pot— perhaps fifty or a hundred—glueing them together and working out the design.

Some pueblo women are still making pots. In almost every village there are a few who make plain kitchenware for their own use. With the Hopi this is quite a common thing. More often the potters make beautiful decorated ware, each in the style of her own village and sell it for ornaments. The following pictures show two famous potters, Maria Martinez of San Ildefonso, and Nampeyo of Hano on Hopi First Mesa, going through the process of grinding clay, then coiling, shaping, and baking the pot.

The Clay. Pueblo women have no materials ready to hand. They have to dig the clay in one place, find sand to mix with it in another, get paint in another. Each village usually has its own clay pit, or more than one, and experts can recognize pots of different pueblos by whether the clay is fine or coarse; mixed with sand or mica. In former days, each woman dug her clay with a stick and carried it home in a basket or hide. While digging, she spoke to the earth, asking permission, and perhaps leaving an offering, for pueblo people feel that clay and rocks, like animals and plants, have their own feelings, and that man must live on kindly terms with them. Today,

Plate IV-1. Maria Martinez of San Ildefonso grinding clay for pottery

women dig with a metal pick and carry the clay home in gunny sacks. Often they have a man with a wagon or car to drive them, but many still speak to the earth as they used to do.

After the clay has been brought home, the potter has days of work ahead of her. She must pound the hard lumps fine and take out the pebbles. Then she may grind the clay on a stone, just as she grinds cornmeal, until it is soft and fine. The picture shows Maria ready to grind. She has water in the pot beside her, for moistening the lumps, so that grinding will be easier. If she does not mean to use the clay right away, the potter wraps it in a damp cloth to keep it from hardening again. Sometimes she buries it in the ground, where it will not dry out so easily.

The next step is to mix the fine clay with some gritty material which will coarsen the texture and allow air bubbles to escape so that they do not burst or blister the pot while baking. This added grit is called temper. Maria and the other Tewa women use volcanic sand which they find nearby and so do their Keresan neighbors in the Rio Grande Valley, at Domingo and Cochiti. Santa Ana and Zia pound up volcanic rock; Zuni and Acoma pound up old pottery scraps; Hopi, Taos, and Picuris have clay which needs no temper at all.

Plate IV-2. Nampeyo of Hano, building the jar

The potter knows from experience about how much temper she will need—
a fistful to a basket of clay or some such measure.

Building the Jar.   In the picture above, you see a potter building
her jar and plate IV-3, steps 1, 2, and 3 give a picture of the steps.   In front
of her she has an old bowl which you see clearly in the picture and at B in
diagram 1.   It will serve as a mold and support for the new jar she is starting.
First she moistens her hands, so they will slip easily over the clay.   The potter
in this case has her water in a pail which you can barely see behind her and
the clay on a cloth before her. She puts a lump of moist clay into the supporting jar and flattens it with her fist until it is molded to the curve of the other
vessel. This will form the base of the new jar. In the picture, the supporting
jar is rather deep so that the base of the new one will be molded for several
inches.   In the diagram, it is a mere plate and the clay is a pancake with the
edges turned. (figure 2) This differs in different pueblos.

Next comes the building of the jar beyond the support.   The potter
pinches the edge of her base until it is thin and irregular, as the picture
shows.   This leaves room for the next coil of clay and some irregularities
for it to stick to.   Now she takes a handful of clay and rolls it between her
hands into a long sausage.   This she lays along the edge, on the inside, as in

73

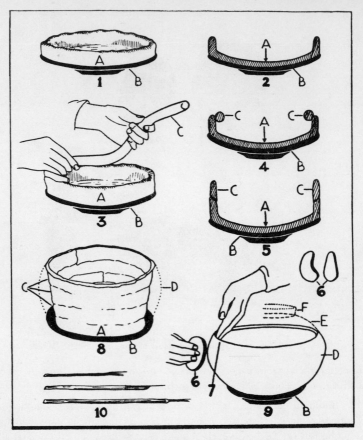

Plate IV-3. Nine steps in building a jar

figures 3 and 4, pinching it into place with her fingers (figure 3). Then she adds another roll and another, turning the jar and its support so that she is always working on the near side. This helps to keep the curve regular, even without a potter's wheel.

She does not try to give the sides of her jar the proper bulge at this first stage but builds them up straight, like a pail. (figure 8) Later she will round and thin them to the exact shape. If the jar she is making is a small one, she works straight ahead until it has reached the proper height. If it is large, the soft clay will not hold up and she has to let it dry every now and then. Usually she works on several pots at once, so that she can add new coils to one, while the others are drying. She must watch the drying ones too and keep their edges moistened or the new clay will not stick.

Plate IV-4. Building and thinning the sides

     With big pots, she stops to do some shaping and thinning every now and then. With small ones, she may leave this process till the end. Scraping and shaping is one of the most skilled tasks in pottery making, for it means giving the pot its distinctive curve, and reducing its thick and lumpy walls to an even thinness. The tools used are little pieces of hard gourd shell, cut so that their edges have different curves, to fit any shape of pot. In the picture, you see Maria Martinez, who has built her pot up straight and is now going to push out its walls until they swell like the two finished pots in front of her. At her right lie the different pieces of gourd shell. With these, she scrapes and smooths the sides of the pots, until they are thin and even. Meantime, her left hand, inside the pot, is gently pushing the walls outward (figure 9 in plate IV-3). The motion must be slow and gentle, the right hand outside the pot always pressing against the left hand inside, so that the walls will not crack.

     All the time she works, she is wetting the clay so it will shape properly and wetting her fingers so they will not stick to it. Now the damp pot must dry and stiffen before she can go further with it. She sets it in the shade, since the sun of the Southwest would dry it too fast, and it might crack. If

75

the weather is rainy, she sets it indoors. It must dry for a day or two and if a little crack develops meantime she can mend it with damp clay. Big cracks are hopeless and when she sees one she breaks the vessel up and begins over again.

If the pot has dried safely, she can give it its final smoothing before the decoration. This is done with something sharp, once a flake of stone or a broken piece of pottery, now a metal knife. With this she scrapes all knobby and thick places and if the pot looks thin somewhere she adds a bit of damp clay. With cooking pots this is the last step before firing, but with decorated pots, there is plenty more to do.

Slipping. The gritty surface of the pot is too rough for painting, so the potter gives it a layer of fine, soft, special clay, without any temper. This is called the slip and is usually white or red. Clay fine enough for a slip can be found only in certain places and women prize their supplies of it and pay high for them in trade.

The potter pounds up her slip clay in a little stone bowl or mortar. Then she mixes it with water to make a thin wash and wipes it onto the pot with a piece of buckskin, fur, or, in these days, a rag. She puts on several coats, letting the pot dry between times and if she wants the color very clear the coats may be as many as five or six. The color of the slip and the way it is put on is one of the chief points of difference in the pottery of the different pueblos. Some, as later pictures will show, cover a pot almost to the bottom. Some leave a wide, unslipped base. Some slip bowls both inside and outside and some only on one or the other.

Even this soft, untempered clay does not leave the pot surface smooth enough. While the slip is still damp, the potter rubs it with a smooth, water-worn pebble, whose curve is just right for that particular pot. She treasurers this pebble and a number of others in varying shapes as a modern carpenter might cherish a set of fine chisels. True, she did not buy them, but she, like her mother and grandmother before her, is always on the lookout for smooth, evenly curved stones and in the course of many generations, they have made a collection suitable for large pots, for small, for incurves, for outcurves, and straight sides. Gently and patiently she rubs her pebble all over the jar until the surface is so shiny that white purchasers often think it has a coat of some glassy material, as modern china has. They do not know the hours of work that go into this polishing. It is a job which a woman willingly hands over to her daughter or any other helper. Some, it is said, help out the polish by rubbing with a greasy rag but most do the work with their own muscle. The result is such a soft luster that it is unfortunate the jars are not waterproof, even after they are fired.

Painting. After the slip, comes painting. The colors, of which we will say more later, are usually red and black. The potter pounds them to

Plate IV-5. Zuni potter painting her design on the white slip before firing the jar

powder in a mortar, mixes them with water and keeps them in little pots, sometimes four pots made all in one piece. Her brushes are sections of stiff yucca leaf, with the ends chewed into a fringe, some fine, some coarse. She places her left hand inside the pot and puts on the design with her right, perhaps measuring a little with the eye and fingers to see how she is coming out. Skilled artists come out evenly, poor ones have to crowd the design but none of them sketch it in beforehand. Each potter has her characteristic patterns which, perhaps have come down from her mother and her mother's mother.

In fact, each village has its typical designs and its rules of style, and all that the individual potter does, in many cases, is to combine the traditional lines and curves in her own special way. (Plate IV-5)

Below is a list of the materials used in pottery, which differ among the many different pueblos according to the clay they can get and the colors they prefer.

Clay. Clay must be sedimentary clay, not adobe which falls apart and does not smooth easily. The deposits of sedimentary clay are usually a coarse red (used by Cochiti, Tesuque, Domingo, Zia, Santa Ana, Jemez, San Ildefonso). Acoma clay is finer and bakes hard. Zuni clay is a blackish gray. Hopi has a coarse, porous clay which needs no temper. Taos and Picuris have clay containing particles of mica, which also needs no temper.

Temper. The Rio Grande pueblos, San Juan, Santa Clara, Santo Domingo, and Cochiti use volcanic sand, which they can dig in the neighboring hills. Santa Ana and Zia, on Santa Ana Creek, get volcanic rock which they pound up. Acoma and Zuni pound up old pottery scraps. Taos, Picuris, and Hopi have clays with sufficient grit in them so that no temper is needed. Hopi, however, uses temper for its plain cooking pots though not for the decorative pots which are sold.

Colors. The white slip is kaolin, of varying degrees of purity. Some pueblos have beds of a finer, more cream colored clay called bentonite. The red is ochre, which usually looks rust colored or brownish. Acoma, however, has recently found beds of this material which burn to a brighter red or even orange.

Black paint is made in several ways. The most usual is to boil down the green stems of the Rock Mountain beeplant. The syrup forms a gluey mass and finally hardens into a cake which can be kept for years. When used, it is ground up and mixed with water like clay. Domingo uses a fine cream slip on which this paint shows black without any mixture. Zuni, Acoma, and Zia mix it with a black mineral containing iron and manganese. Hopi boils down the stems of tansy mustard and mixes them with an iron compound found in the neighborhood.

The most beautiful and shiny black is not made with paint but by smudging the whole pot with smoke. This is done at San Ildefonso, Santa Clara, and San Juan.

Firing. The jar will soon crumble unless it is hardened in the fire. Modern manufacturers of dishes have special furnaces for this purpose but the pueblo woman builds her own each time: walls, firebox, and floor. She chooses a windless day, so that the fire will keep an even heat, but even then she is nervous. There is almost no way to be sure that a pot will come through safely, for some little change in the temper, the clay, or the heat may bring about a crack which will ruin the labor of days.

Early morning is the best time for firing, because the wind often comes up in the afternoon. The woman clears a space on the ground, builds a little fire, and sets the pots around it to get gradually warm. This will help to prevent cracks when they are really baking. When this preliminary fire has burned out, she starts to build her oven. First, she makes the floor on which the pots are to stand. In the old days, this was done with broken pieces of large pots raised on stones. Now the women use tin cans standing on end, helped out by scraps of iron or any piece of grating they can find. In the picture, (see frontispiece) Maria Martinez has placed a number of cans and is arranging the warm pots on them upside down. The bulging sides of the pots must not touch or they will be spotted, but the rims may touch and Maria is building a second layer of pots, with their rims on the bases of the first.

Behind her, in a galvanized iron tub, are some sheets of scrap iron, which she will use to build up the walls of the oven around the pots, so the fire shall not touch them. Old scraps of pottery formed the oven roof in early days for then it was not so large, since the women were not making pots for sale. In front of Maria are two tubs of caked cow dung, which is the main fuel. Cattle have been a blessing to the pottery makers, since the dried dung burns so slowly and evenly. Hopi, Zuni, and Acoma use sheep dung which, trodden into cakes in the corral, is just as good. In early days, they had to use wood—all but the Hopi, who found some soft coal in their area, dug it out and used it, just for pottery making. They use a little with the sheep dung still. Maria fits more cakes of cow dung over the sheets of iron which form the roof of her oven, so that the fire is above the pots as well as below them.

At the left of the cow dung is the pile of cedar bark which Maria uses for kindling. This will be pushed in under the pots and lit. Slowly the manure will catch fire and the potter has nothing more to do but to wait and hope that no wind will come up. She does not have to add more fuel for she has used the right amount to burn for as long as she needs—half an hour for the smallest pots and up to as much as two hours for larger ones. She has put in pots that are about of a size so the heat will be right for all of them. When the fire has burned out, the pots will be done, though sometimes she may poke aside the fuel and look at them to make sure how things are going. If she feels convinced, by the red hue of the pots, that they have had enough she will pull the fire apart. After the fire has burned out, the potter often leaves the pots in the oven all night, so that they may cool slowly. Otherwise, she pushes the sheets of iron aside and carefully removes the pots with sticks, setting them upside down to cool.

Firing Black Pottery. Under the subject of paint, we referred briefly to the firing of black pottery by smudging it with smoke. Plate IV-6 shows Maria and Julian Martinez, who are famous for the process, just after having covered their fire for this purpose. The fire and the oven were, at first

Plate IV-6. Firing black pottery

prepared like any other. The pots, painted with a red slip, were baked for about half an hour. San Juan potters, who specialize in all-red ware, would have removed them at that time. Maria, instead, has left them in place and smothered the fire with dry manure. Behind her is a pile of ashes which she sometimes adds in order to keep the smoke in. The carbon in the heavy black smoke will settle on the jars, coloring them permanently. The polishing they have had gives a beautiful sheen, like jet.

Waterproofing. The pottery process we have described is the very oldest, used by the early people of Europe, Egypt, and Assyria before the wheel, the furnace, and the glassy outside coat or glaze were invented. Until the time of glaze, no jars could be completely waterproof, and pueblo jars are not. It is true that the longer they are polished and the hotter the baking fire, the less porous they will be, but clay with its temper makes a surface full of tiny holes and drops will find their way through it. Pueblo women did not mind this, especially with jars meant to hold drinking water, for the drops evaporated on the outside of the jar and kept the water on the inside cool. If water had to be carried long distances, when evaporation would have been a waste, the potter made a small-mouthed jar and coated the inside with melted pinyon gum. Her food dishes held grease, which ultimately soaked into the clay and sealed it. White purchasers, who buy pueblo pots to hold flowers, give the inner wall a coat of spar varnish or set a glass inside them.

Otherwise, the outer polish is ruined by seeping water and the higher the polish the worse the result, as with the lustrous red or black ware of the Tewa.

Shapes. The shapes of pots are more or less the same for all the pueblos. Mostly, they are simple jars and bowls for the covers, handles, plates, and figurines sold now have often been developed in response to the tourist trade. Women are adding numberless new shapes, such as candlesticks, bookends, and ashtrays.

Styles. These shapes, all but the bric-a-brac for sale, have been used by the pueblos for a thousand years and more. Colors, too, have remained the same, for the standbys were red and white clay, with black obtained in

Plate IV-7. Most customary shapes of Pueblo pottery, (from left to right) large storage jar, tall water jar, bowl, smaller water jar, small mouthed water jar, shallow bowl

various ways. Yet each region had a variation of its own and sometimes kept the same style for a hundred years. Perhaps the women of those days were proud of their inherited patterns and perhaps they saw less of other villages than they do now. At any rate, students have found they can use these standard types of pottery to follow the journeyings of different pueblo groups. They can see where a new group joined an old one and brought another style. They can tell when a group split away from their friends and carried the old style to new places. They see foreign pieces and guess at trade with Mexico and southern Arizona. In fact, this habit of keeping to one style in pottery has been one of our chief helps in working out pueblo history. Experts examine the color and design of a pot, the shape, even the clay, temper, and kind of firing. Usually they can tell the period when a pot was made, the region where it was made, and perhaps the very pueblo.

They do the same today. Only twelve pueblos now make pottery, yet under the stimulus of sale they have developed some forty styles. New ones are constantly appearing or old ones being revived. The New Mexico Association for Indian Affairs, which gives prizes every year for the best pots,

1. Black on Cream:
   Santo Domingo, Cochiti, Tesuque.
2. Three Colored:
   Santa Ana, Zia, Acoma, Zuni, Laguna.
3. Black on Mottled Orange:
   Hopi First Mesa.
4. Polished Black or Polished Red:
   Santa Clara, San Juan, San Ildefonso.
5. Unpainted:
   Taos, Picuris.
6. Modern Variegated:
   Santa Clara, San Juan, San Ildefonso, Tesuque.

Plate IV-8. Map of pueblo country, showing modern pottery areas

has to give one prize for old style and one for new. Still, the styles fall into groups just as did those of earlier days.

The list with the map above sorts out these groups by color for the ordinary observer. Temper and clay are not considered, since these require scientific analysis. However, the list of materials on page 86 will show that pueblos using the same general style often have access to the same clay, temper, and paint. Nor is shape considered in the list because most all pueblos have nearly all shapes. In any village, you can find jars ranging from squatty to slender, bowls deep or shallow. Where some form like the Hopi bowl has become a noticeable specialty, that is mentioned in the later descriptions. There have been many recent changes.

On the map, the pueblos using the same general style are enclosed by a dotted line. It is interesting to see that such pueblos do not necessarily

NEW MEXICO

5 TAOS
PICURIS
4 SAN JUAN
SANTA CLARA POJOAQUE
SAN ILDEFONSO NAMBE
6 TESUQUE
Santa Fe
1
JEMEZ COCHITI
ZIA SANTO DOMINGO
SANTA ANNA SAN FELIPE
SANDIA
San Jose
Albuquerque
2 LAGUNA
ACOMA ISLETA

Map by E. H. Coulson, BIA

speak the same language. Rather, they occupy the same river valley or general kind of country. Perhaps their women found the same materials and perhaps, too, they had a good chance to see one another's pots, no matter what language they spoke.

The pages following contain pictures and descriptions of the styles used in all villages active in pottery making. They do not include San Felipe, Sandia, Pojoaque, Jemez, Isleta, and Santa Ana, which have dropped pottery for other pursuits. Among the others, notice the changes! Hopi and San Ildefonso have revolutionized their former styles. Many of the Tewa are trying several fashions, new and old. Scarcely a pueblo is making the very same ware as when they were first studied about 1870. Indian art is moving and the pottery scraps show that, although the change is slow, there has always been change.

83

Plate IV-9. Black on cream, Santo Domingo

1. BLACK ON CREAM

Santo Domingo

Color. The slip is bentonite, a cream colored clay so fine that it can be polished with a rag instead of a stone. Decoration in rich black, made from the Rocky Mountain beeplant without mineral addition. Within recent years a little red has been added to the design.

Design. The figures are mostly geometrical, made by drawing bands of squares or rectangles and then cutting off the corners with angular or curving masses of black color. The result is large, widely spaced black triangles, often with one curving side. Newer designs are large plant and bird forms containing red. Very recently the village has been making a great quantity of polished black ware, in imitation of San Ildefonso. This ware is a rusty black with typical flower and geometrical motifs.

History. The black-on-cream style has been in use for a century or two. Before that Domingo used decorations of glossy black mineral glaze on red. It was pre-Spanish but may have taken some hints from the Spaniards and therefore was given up after the pueblo revolution in 1680.

Plate IV-10. Black on cream, Cochiti

1. BLACK ON CREAM

Cochiti

Colors. The slip is bentonite, its color a pinkish cream in the newer pieces, yellowish white in older ones. It extends unusually close to the base, sometimes all the way. Designs in black outline.

Design. This pueblo, unlike the others, has no taboo against representing symbols of fertility, such as clouds, rain and lightning. There are also fantastic bird, human, and animal forms, scattered at random over the cream surface, with the effect of line drawings.

Distinctive Shapes. A good many animal and human figurines.

History. The black-on-cream style with its fertility symbols and bird and animal forms goes back for a century and perhaps two. At some time before that the style was black glaze on red as with Domingo.

85

Plate IV-11. Black on cream, Tesuque

1. BLACK ON CREAM

Tesuque

Colors.   The bentonite slip is a grayish cream, showing crackling as a result of firing.   The crackling serves to distinguish this ware from that of Cochiti whose colors are otherwise similar. Decoration in black outlines.

Design.   Wavy black lines circle the pot which is not divided into separate design fields.   Often there is a meander or "Greek key" design, which breaks at intervals into three or five lobed leaves.   This style differs from that of Cochiti, which also use black outlines, in that there are few human and animal forms.

History.   This is the style characteristic of pueblo since about 1700. Since it does not appeal to white purchasers, it has been almost completely given up in favor of tourist bric-a-brac, tinted with commercial colors.   (See page 105) Some women occasionally produce jars in the old style, in response to prizes offered by the New Mexico Association for Indian Affairs.

Plate IV-12. Three colored pottery, Santa Ana

2. THREE COLORED

Santa Ana

Colors. The kaolin slip is grayish white because of impurities and is generally much worn, since most pieces are old. The red base extends far up the jar, sometimes to the shoulder. Decoration is red figures outlined or partly outlined with black.

Design. Bold, crude figures, generally thick bands in terrace formation.

History. Pottery is no longer made at this pueblo, though twenty years ago there were women still working. Even the few old pieces now to be found are carelessly and poorly executed.

Plate IV-13. Three colored pottery, Zia

2. THREE COLORED

Zia

Colors. The slip is white which, in some recent cases, has been changed to buff. The base of the jar is slipped in red for some distance up the sides. Decoration is in red ochre and black made from rocks containing iron and manganese ground fine and mixed with juice from the Rocky Mountain beeplant as glue. Occasionally the red is omitted.

Design. There is more variety of design than in many other pueblos. The most distinctive pattern represents a long-legged bird with a few big tail feathers. Often there is a wide curved band in heavy red. Other designs are fawns, plant sprays, conventionalized leaves, and some geometric forms.

History. Zia, in early days, was a great style center and its influence on other pueblos may be noticed, as occasionally at Acoma. At present, pottery is dying out, since the pueblo is so far from the highway that there is little opportunity for sale.

88

Plate IV-14. Three colored pottery, Acoma

2. THREE COLORED

Acoma

Colors. The kaolin slip is white to yellow cream, with deep base of red or dark brown. The decorations are in red and black, or occasionally black only. Up to a hundred years ago, the red was of only one dark shade. Since then, various beds of ochre have been discovered, which bake yellow, orange, red, and brown.

Design. There are two main types of design. One is an allover pattern, covering the whole jar with complicated angles and curves. The other, influenced by Zia, has a few large flowers or birds. The Acoma bird can usually be distinguished by his curved, parrot-like beak.

Distinctive Structure. Acoma pottery is recognized by its thinness. The jars are finer and lighter than those of other pueblos.

History. Acoma styles have changed less since they were first studied in 1870 than those of almost any other pueblo. Even the influence from Zia seems to have been quite early.

Plate IV-15. Three colored pottery, Zuni

2. THREE COLORED

Zuni

Colors.   Slip, clear white kaolin, which darkens with age.   It does not extend quite to the base of the jar, the lower part being slipped with brown or black. Decorations in black, with touches of red.

Design.   The surface to be decorated is laid off in sections, usually two or four, each of which contains a unit design, such as a deer, a bird, or rosette. The neck has a smaller, geometrical pattern of its own. It is separated from the body by a band, often a double black line, which must always be broken at one point, as a "spirit path."   Otherwise, the belief is that the maker's soul would be imprisoned and she might die.

Distinctive Shapes.   Zuni water jars are made on a bowl foundation and often show a bulge where the sides spread out beyond this.   Zuni specialized in the pottery owl, though all pueblos made bird forms sometimes.

History.   Zuni pots have kept to the old style more nearly than many of the others, though they have changed slowly since 1879. Very few are made now.

90

Plate IV-16. Black on mottled orange, Hopi

3. BLACK ON MOTTLED ORANGE

Hopi

(First Mesa)

Colors. The slip is of clay, the same kind as that in the jar and when it is fired, shows mottling which ranges from orange to cream, depending on how little air gets to it. The decorations are in black (or dark brown), reddish orange, and white. Less frequently, the slip is dark red, decorated with black or black and white.

Design. The design is spreading and unsymmetrical, and contains curving lines which are often a conventionalization of feathers and bird forms. The mottled background is an important part of the decoration.

Distinctive Shapes. The jar is unusually squat, with flattened shoulder and small mouth. The bowl has an incurving rim.

History. Before 1859, decorated pottery had almost ceased on the Hopi mesas. Then Nampeyo, a Tewa woman of Hano, adopted the designs of pottery dug up by archaeologists at the ruined village of Sikyatki. Other First Mesa women, both Hopi and Tewa, have followed her.

91

Plate IV-17. Polished black or polished red, Santa Clara

4. POLISHED BLACK OR POLISHED RED

Santa Clara

Colors. The slip is originally red but can be turned black if the flame is smothered as described on page 87. This pueblo uses mostly the black style.

Design. Usually the decoration comes only from the high polish given to the black surface by painstaking rubbing. On large jars, the potter may press into the soft clay a five pointed mark, commonly called the bear paw. Since 1930, women have been experimenting with designs of matte (lusterless) black on polished black like those invented at San Ildefonso. They have also gone further and carved designs on platters which are fired either black or red. The depressions on the carving are painted with matte color, while the relief is polished.

Distinctive Shapes. There are an unusual number of double-mouthed jars, the two mouths connected by a strap handle. Although this form is made occasionally in the other pueblos, Santa Clara specializes in making it for sale. It is commonly known as a wedding jar and bride and groom are supposed to drink from it at the same time. The pueblo also makes clever animal figurines, which are molded with the fingers, not coiled.

History. The polished black is an old style in Tewa country, which has recently become popular to the exclusion of others.

Plate IV-18. Polished black or polished red, San Juan

4. POLISHED BLACK OR POLISHED RED

San Juan

Colors. The slip is originally red but can be turned black if the flame is smothered. San Juan prefers the red style. This pueblo also slips and polishes a smaller portion of the jar than Santa Clara. The slip may extend only half way down the sides or only to the shoulder, leaving a deep unpolished base. With bowls, only the interior may be slipped and polished, or only the exterior.

Design. The only decoration is little lumps of clay sometimes added to the jar to form warlike projections. (San Juan, Taos, and Picuris are the only pueblos which decorate by adding clay instead of painting. San Juan is nearest of the Tewa to these northern Tiwa and though its polished pottery is otherwise very different from their plain ware, this may be a case of influence.)

93

Plate IV-19. Polished black or polished red and older black on cream, San Ildefonso

4. POLISHED BLACK OR POLISHED RED

San Ildefonso

Colors. The slip originally red but can be turned black if the fire is smothered while it is baking. Eighty percent of San Ildefonso ware is black. On the polished surface is usually a design in the same color but without luster. This is produced by first polishing the red slip and then applying a design in paint made of pinkish gray stone. If the pot is fired red, this design appears in deeper red, if black, in luster black.

Design. The figures are usually angular and geometric. Sometimes the flowing form of the plumed serpent surrounds a bowl or plate. In some of the newer products the design is **carved** into the clay instead of painted on.

Distinctive Shapes. A round platter, not used in former times, is popular among white buyers, as are small decorative jars and ash trays.

History. The dull black on polished black, although now nationally famous dates only from 1919. At that time, San Ildefonso pottery was black with some red. There were a few old pieces of polished black, made by the smothering method. Maria Martinez, a skilled potter, experimented with this style and her husband Julian helped her. White specialists in Santa Fe encouraged them and they devised the dull (matte) black design in a polished background. They have demonstrated their work at museums and exhibitions all over the country. Maria now has several women to help her and they sometimes coil and polish the pots while she puts on the finishing touches. Julian applies the design, one of the few men in the pueblos to be connected with pottery making.

94

Plate IV-20. Unpainted pottery, Taos and Picuris

5. UNPAINTED

Taos, Picuris

Colors. This clay has no slip. It is of a brownish color which bakes to a mottled tan, sometimes almost golden. The potters often allow fire blemishes which show bluish splotches. Occasionally they smother the fire as at Santa Clara and turn the whole pot black. The clay is filled with tiny particles of mica (which substitute for temper so that temper is not used) and these show on the baked surface as glittering specks.

Design. There is no painted decoration. Sometimes the necks of the vessels are trimmed with a rope of clay, attached by pressing it against the damp jar with the fingers and then baking it on.

Distinctive Shapes. Unlike the usual squatty pueblo jar, these shapes are tall and thin with small bases. Recently, they have had handles and covers.

History. This style is entirely different from that of the other pueblos where unpainted ware is made for cooking, but not in these tall shapes and not with applique decoration.

Taos and Picuris, on the edge of the Plains country, have apparently adopted the pottery style of the Navaho, Apache, and of various Plains Indians. Whether or not they ever made painted pottery, like the other pueblos, we do not know.

95

Plate IV-21. Modern Variegated from Santa Clara

6. MODERN VARIEGATED

San Juan, Santa Clara, San Ildefonso, Tesuque

Colors. A number of different styles are spoken of in this section, not because they have much in common but because they are new and do not yet fit any classification. They are evidence of an urge for inventiveness

Plate IV-22. Modern Variegated from San Juan

Plate IV-23. Modern Variegated from San Ildefonso

among the pueblos and also of the importance of the tourist to the present day potter.

Santa Clara.   At Santa Clara and San Juan there has been a search for new clays, perhaps in competition with San Ildefonso whose dull black on polished black has such a good sale. Santa Clara has developed an entirely new color scheme of white and pale red on dull red.

San Juan.   Since 1930 San Juan has been making pots in the natural buff-colored clay, unslipped, but decorated with a band of incised slanting marks around the shoulder. This style is said to come from ancient pottery found in neighboring ruins. Women have added variations of their own to this ancient style. First, the portion of the jar above and below the incised band was given a polished red slip. Then the incised decoration was made in curves with open spaces between them and these were filled in with pink and gray, both new colors for pottery.

San Ildefonso.   This pueblo, now a pottery center with a great variety of wares, is also trying new color schemes. In addition to the popular polished red or polished black, its women make pots slipped with red and painted with designs in white, black and white, or pink outlined with white.

Tesuque.   Tesuque has also developed a new style though, instead of searching for colored clays, its women have invested in commercial poster colors. In contrast to the earth colors, these are of violent bright shades and, since they are applied after the pot is fired, they soon wear off. This venture has no historic derivation and it is unfortunate that it is encouraged by the tourist trade.

97

Chapter V

STONE TOOLS AND WHAT THEY MADE

Tools

WHEN early pueblo men made a trip outside the village, they kept a sharp lookout for choice pieces of stone, their tool material. An alert man might return loaded with selected stones as a modern man brings purchases from the store. Among them would be glasslike chert and jasper for arrowheads; slivers of quartz for knives; heavy diorite for hammers; slabs of sandstone for smoothing the surface of wood. These had to be chipped and shaped into the tools which would make his weapons and much of the household equipment. Each man made his own supply or, at least, had a relative in the house who could make it. He kept desirable stones in his storage room, awaiting the winter days when there would be time for such work.

The tool maker sat down out of doors, where he could get a tough, flat stone to pound on, and plenty of sand for rubbing. He had a jar of water at his side, a round, smooth stone to hammer with, a strip of buckskin to protect his hand while working and, perhaps, a sliver of bone to be used in prying flakes from a stone edge. Few men can do this work now, for pueblo people have had metal for two hundred and fifty years. Still, they have heard about the process and we can make a list of the old stone tools from their memories, from pictures, and from articles dug up in the ruins.

Making stone tools was men's work for it was one of the pueblo rules that a person made the articles he used. Women made their stone-grinding slabs and their piki ovens, even though their husbands might bring the stones home for them. Men made the hammers, knives, and arrows which they would use in skin and woodwork. There were two main kinds of stone tools: those for hammering or striking and those for cutting. The striking tools were made out of heavy stone that did not split easily, like granite or diorite. The toolmaker had been careful to choose lumps of about the size he would need and he chipped these roughly into shape by hammering with another stone. Then came the tiresome business of shaping and polishing. He sprinkled the flat stone at his feet with sand, wet the stone tool, and then rubbed it patiently to and fro, round and round, until it was well shaped and smooth. He could even grind it to a sharp edge, as a farmer grinds a knife with water and whetstone.

The picture shows an axe and a maul or heavy hammer which were shaped in this way. Both have grooves around the top where wooden handles could be tied on. The handle was generally a stick of hard, green wood, split at the top. The two parts of the split section fitted along the groove at each side of the axe head and then were tied together with a leather thong or

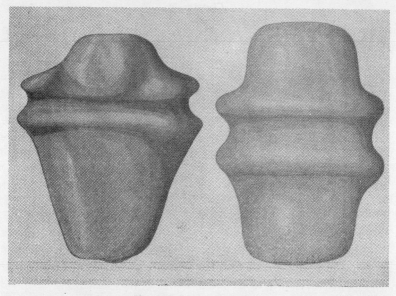

strips of yucca. It does not sound like a powerful tool, yet pueblo men cut down trees (though small ones) and built their roofs with these axes and mauls. At that, they were far ahead of many Indians in the country, for instance those in California, who had no axe at all. You can tell a pueblo axe or maul because the groove goes all the way around the head. Indians further south, in Arizona, made their grooves only three quarters of the way around, and, when the diggers find one of these three quarter axes in the north, they see a picture of early trading and travelling. (Plate V-1)

The cutting tools were made of stone which splits easily, like chert, jasper, quartz, chalcedony or the black, volcanic glass, obsidian. For these the toolmaker again cracked his fragment into shape. These brittle stones always break with a sharp, jagged edge and he sharpened the edge still further. He took a sliver of bone and pressed its point against the stone, near the edge, tapping it lightly until a tiny flake of stone flew off. When a row of these flakes were forced off, close together, they produced an edge which was very faintly scalloped. This was what the ancient pueblo people used for a knife. Usually they made it in triangular shape, iike an arrowhead but about three inches long. They chipped small notches at the base of the triangle, so that handle could be tied on about as an arrow shaft is tied. This knife would do to skin an animal or to take off an enemy's scalp. It would even cut hair and cut out a moccasin pattern but it is no wonder they did not tailor cotton garments with it.

Other cutting tools were arrow points: slender, notched triangles like the knife only half as large. There was also an awl, a longer and slenderer point, triangular in cross section. This was used to make holes in buckskin so that it could be tied together with leather thongs, the substitute for sewing. A heavy stone point, about a foot long was broken and sharpened very roughly. This was the pick to be used in breaking out stone.

Next after stone tools came those made of bone and wood. Men carefully saved the bones of a deer, just as they saved its skin and sinew, for deer bones made excellent tools, with very little shaping. Splinters of bone, with their long sharp ends, made good awls. They were used in basketry and for making holes in buckskin so that it could be tied together with thongs, the old pueblo substitute for sewing. A few even had eyes pierced in them, so that they could be used as needles. A section of deerhorn, eight or ten inches long, was cut off straight across the tip and sharpened for use as a chisel. A long, curved section had its tip sharpened into a point so that it formed a pick. This was the implement used to hack out stone in the early turquoise mines.

Deerhorn was generally smooth and polished on slabs of the fine sandstone so abundant in pueblo country. This was useful on wood, too, and men kept a selection of slabs, of different sizes, in their storerooms.

Wooden Implements. In the course of other chapters, we have already mentioned such wooden implements as the firedrill and weaving tools. Later we shall come upon wood used in the cradle board and the scraping stick. All these were roughly shaped with the stone knife and then rubbed smooth with sandstone. But the most important wooden tool made by any man was his bow.

Weapons

The Bow. It must have been a great day for pueblo people when they learned about this weapon, somewhere about six or seven hundred A.D. Before that, they had only the throwing stick which has to be used in open country where the hunter stands up and raises his arm in full sight of the deer or the enemy. We guess that it was new arrivals in the country who brought the bow and there must have been many a campfire discussion as to whether this modern, complicated instrument with a string that was always breaking was really better than the good old **atlatl.** By the time the white people arrived everybody had taken to the new fashion and the **atlatl** was forgotten.

Self Bow. The first bows were very simple. Parts of them found in the ruins show that they were simple bent strips of hard wood, like that in photograph V-3. The Hopi used such bows until the white people came, and so did many people in the other pueblos. So did most of the Indians in the Southwest and California. It was only the new arrivals, the Navaho and Apache, who had the more complicated bow we shall describe later.

Plate V-2. Cochiti drum maker. Note bows and arrows, also

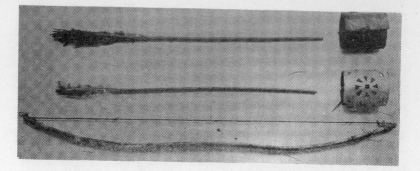

Plate V-3. Hopi bow, arrows and wristguards

A man making a self bow cut a strong sapling of oak, yew, mountain mahogany, or juniper and if possible, tried to get one that had grown in a curved position. He cut a length about three and a half to four and a half feet long, depending on whether he himself was tall or short. He scraped it with a stone knife so that it was thickest at the middle, where his hand would grasp it, and tapered a little toward the ends. At each end he cut a notch to hold the bowstring.

If the wood had no curve, he might lay it over hot ashes, steam it soft, and then tie it in the bent shape he wanted. Some men, however, preferred to leave the rod straight and pull it into a curve with the bowstring. That gave it more snap, they said. The last touch was to rub the wood for a long time with sandstone to make it smooth, and perhaps to rub a special hollow where the grasping fingers would come.

Sinew-Backed Bow. Some of the pueblos, especially the Keres, made a more complicated bow. This was the type called "sinew backed," used by Navaho and Apache. Many Tiwa and Tewa had it, and even the Zuni preferred it when they had to kill enemies instead of deer. "But there was much discussion among the old people," the pueblos report, "as to whether it was really any better." This sinew-backed bow was shorter than the self bow, for it was developed by people who had very little wood and had to make up with extra materials for the lack of tall, springy saplings. It was used, too, by people who rode horseback and could not bother with a long bow. This bow is the weapon of the Eskimo, of some Plains Indians, and the wandering horseback riding tribes of Asia.

A sinew-backed bow was cut and whittled like a simple one, except that the maker sometimes bent it into the double curve which whites call Cupid's bow. Then he cut long strips of sinew and glued them to the back with pinyon gum or, later, a paste made of boiled wheat grains. This kept the wood from breaking and adding to its spring. He made this backing extra strong by winding sinew around the bow crosswise. Often he wrapped a piece of buckskin around the middle of the bow, where his hand would grip it.

The bowstring was made of sinew, generally the long strips from the leg of a deer. A man split off two strands with his teeth, wet them, and rolled them together on his leg just as he spun cotton. He wound the string tightly to the bow at one end and fastened the other with a half hitch which could be loosened when the bow was not in use. If the sinew were kept taut all the time it would stretch and lose its spring. In fact, a bowstring needed constant attention, for it loosened when the weather was wet, tightened and perhaps snapped when it was dry. Most men kept their bows in some sort of case and kept extra strings handy. They needed these when the war chief made a yearly inspection of weapons, as he did in so many pueblos. He tried every bow and if a string broke people thought pretty badly of the owner.

Arrows. Arrows were of various kinds also. The simplest were made by anybody who could get straight pieces of hard wood,—sumac (Rhus trilobata), oak (Quercus gambelli), or wild currant (Ribes inebrians), about eighteen to twenty-six inches long. Some of the Tiwa say they looked for stems which were not curved but had a jog in them for then the arrow flew straight but was hard to pull out. The maker scraped off the bark, then smoothed and evened the shafts by rubbing with sandstone. If the sticks needed straightening he steamed them over the fire till they were pliable, then passed them through a hole in a piece of horn with which he could pull them into shape. Then he rubbed them smooth on sandstone. He generally made a groove lengthwise of the arrow and he painted it with some distinctive mark, so that he would recognize it sticking in a deer or enemy.

If the arrow was to be used for small animals, he might not put a stone tip on it, for tips were expensive—that is, they took a long time to make. Besides they made too big a hole in the skin and flesh. In that case, he merely smoothed the wood to a point with a sharp stone. He made his stone tips out of hard, flaky stone, like chalcedony, obsidian, jasper, chert, slate. They were usually of the shape which had a projection at the bottom. He split the hard wood of the arrow a little way, pushed this projection into it and squeezed in a little melted pinyon gum. Then he wrapped the place tightly around the outside with wet sinew. The sinew would shrink when it was dry and hold very tight. For the feathers he split hawk plumes down the middle of the quill. He cut off the pointed end of the feather with his stone knife and then evened the remainder so that it was the same width all the way. He laid three of these lengthwise along the rear end of the arrow and attached them with sinew. At the very end of the arrow shaft he cut a notch where it would fit into the bowstring.

Pueblo people who lived where they could get reeds (Phragmites communis) used these for their arrows and considered them much better because so much lighter. However, the reed is too fragile to hold a stone tip or a notch in the end, so they had to add pieces of hard wood. They cut the reed shaft longer than wood, since it was lighter. The cut at the end near the tip was planned to come just beyond one of the joints of the reed so that this end had a hard ring where the joint was and then something like a shallow cup which was the beginning of the next section of reed. Into this cup the arrow maker thrust a six-inch stick of hard wood, whittled so that its end would just fit. He gummed it with pinyon gum and also made a wrapping of sinew around the outside of the reed to hold it. This hardwood stick, or fore-shaft, could be sharpened, or it could hold a stone tip, just like a hardwood arrow.

At the lower end of the reed, where the notch should come, the arrow maker made a similar cut near a joint and thrust in a small plug of hardwood like a cork. Then he cut the notch in this.

It can be seen that arrows meant hard work and that they were valuable property. Each man marked his own so that he would recognize them and he tried to get back all that he had shot, whether they were on the ground or in a wounded animal. Arrows were favorite stakes in betting and, on slack days, the young men would shoot at a mark and bet arrows on their success.

Besides his bow and arrow a man made several other weapons, some of which served as tools also. There was, of course, the curved throwing stick, used in the rabbit hunt. This was a thin, flat piece of wood, hacked from a branch which was already curved, then rubbed fine and smooth with sandstone. The curve was said to imitate that of the hawk's wing, for it was the hawk who first taught men to use this stick, which he carried concealed under his wing. Sometimes the owner painted his stick with marks meant to symbolize a face, as in photograph V-4. This is a Hopi stick and the small parallel marks at either end are "his eyes." A man might also cut himself a wooden club from a short strong branch of oak or other hard wood, with a knot in the end. He polished this also on sandstone.

Work In Skins

The Use of Skins. In every pueblo the hunt brought in a good many buckskins and some of the tougher hides of antelope. These were used for clothing. Mountain lion, mountain sheep, wildcat, and coyote skins served for bags, caps, and extra foot wrappings. The soft, furry skin of the red fox was worn whole in ceremonials, as it is today. Usually a few buffalo hides or portions of hide were brought in from the yearly hunt or from trade. These made the best possible bedding for lying on a cold earthen floor, and as they wore out they were cut up piecemeal for moccasin soles, bowguards, and anything else that required heavy skin.

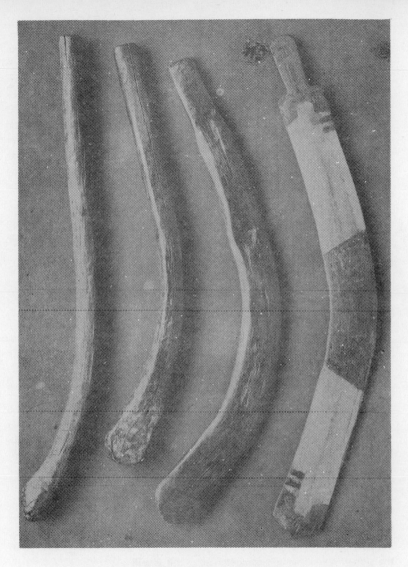

Plate V-4. Hopi throwing sticks

The men did the skin work, both hide dressing and sewing. On the Plains, from which they learned much of their leathercraft in later years, such work was left to the women. But Plains women did not have to grind corn. Pueblo men had done the leather work in former days, when it meant only tying a few skins crudely together, and they kept on, even though they

Plate V-5. Dehairing a buckskin

had to sew the elaborate knee-length moccasins worn by the women. In fact, in many pueblos, making moccasins for the girl he was to marry came to be the sign of a young man's competence, and it is still.

Dressing Buckskin.   Buckskin was the one they worked with oftenest, and many c.d men still know how to treat it in the old way. First the skin was soaked in water for a week to soften it. If the worker could, he soaked it in some outdoor pool.   Otherwise he dampened the hide and buried it in the ground, which kept the moisture just as well.

When the hide was thoroughly soft, he laid it over a tree trunk for scraping. There were several such scraping boards in every pueblo, made of a thick section of cottonwood trunk, five or six feet long, peeled and smoothed. One end was cut slanting so that it would lean at an angle against the wall. The other was cut to fit the ground and perhaps it had branches, cut off short to serve as legs. (Plate V-5)

The skin scraper, in very old days, was probably a long flat piece of some flinty stone, chipped along one edge. The scraper which pueblo people remember now was a drawknife of iron, which they made cleverly for themselves, perhaps after seeing the Spanish tools. They took any thin flat piece of iron they could find, sharpened one edge on a piece of sandstone and set it into a semi-circular handle. This was made of a slender oak rod, steamed in the fire to a half moon shape, about six inches across, with straight ends extending out at the sides as handles. (Plate V-5)

With this tool, and perhaps others of various sizes, the worker removed all scraps of flesh from the skin, then turned it over and removed the hair and the grain (the layer of skin under the hair). Modern leatherworkers often leave the grain, but for a genuine buckskin tan, say pueblo people, it must be scraped off.

Any skinworker already had deer brains boiled and put away. These were removed as soon as an animal was killed, boiled a short time, then wrapped in cornhusk so they would keep. The worker soaked the skin again so it would be soft. If the time were winter, he would take it out early in the morning so it would freeze and then thaw—a specially convenient way of softening. Then he stretched it out to work on. He might tie it to one of the racks of poles which stood outside pueblo houses to hold wood or drying vegetables. He might peg it out on the ground with wooden pegs, though in that case, it would need to be turned during the work. When it was firmly stretched, he began rubbing the oily brains into it on both sides, keeping on until the brains were used up. All the Southwest Indians tanned skins with this sort of oiling and did not smoke them, nor did they use tan bark before the white people came. The skins treated with brains are beautifully soft but not waterproof. When wet they turn stiff and have to be pulled and stretched for re-softening. Pueblo tanners are now experimenting with neatsfoot oil and other modern products but they find that old colorings do not take so well without the oil of animal brains.

After the oiling, the extra moisture had to be taken out of the skin. The worker doubled it around a smooth, upright post, twisted a stick in the hanging ends of the skin for a handle and then wrung it violently as women wring clothes in their hands after washing. The skin was finally dry but out of shape and full of wrinkles. Then the worker rubbed it in both hands to bring back its flexibility. Finally he laid it over his knee and rubbed it patiently with a piece of sandstone, to take off any little roughnesses.

107

After the Spaniards came, pueblo people learned a vegetable tanning method, but they suited it to their own conditions and to the plants they could find. The European way was to boil powdered oak bark, and soak the skins in vats of this liquid for two or three weeks. Pueblo people who could not often get oak, used white fir (Abies concolor), canyaigre (Rumex hymenosepalus), or Mormon tea (Ephedra nevadensis). They dried the bark of the trees or whole stems of the plants in the sun, then boiled and pounded them to powder. They mixed two parts of this liquid with one part of water and soaked a skin in a pot or other clean container which had no metal about it, airing the skin each day so that the acid would not eat into it. Finally it was rinsed in clear water and hung up to dry.

Coloring. A buckskin finished by this process came out white and, to whiten it further, the skinworker rubbed it with a thin wash of white clay of the same kind his wife used for painting her pots. This was generally done after the skin had been made into a garment. Occasionally he might rub parts of a shirt or leggings with yellow clay, red clay, or the copper sulphate which make turquoise blue. The most usual color for skin garments, especially men's moccasins, was a brownish red, a shade which is still worn. If possible, this was a dye made with mountain mahogany. The skin was laid with the side where the hair had been, uppermost, and wood ashes, generally juniper, were sprinkled over it and rubbed in with a corncob. Roots of mountain mahogany (Cerocarpus montanus) were cut up and boiled and the liquid spread over the skin. Then dry pieces of alder bark (Alnus incana) were scattered on it. Without these, the skinworkers say, the mahogany dye would lie in patches and would not soak through the skin. The skin was folded up, hair side in, and left all night. The side treated had a fast, red dye.

The Zuni used another recipe. They boiled the root (Holodiscus dumosus) with a little Indian paint brush (Castillea integra) and dipped the skin in this. Then they added ground up alder bark and dipped it a third time. After this, they rubbed it with wood ashes and then with a corncob to work the red well in.

For black, the Zuni boiled sumac stems and leaves, and when the liquid was cool dipped the buckskin in it. They emptied the bowl twice and filled it with fresh dye. In the third clean bowlful they put a handful of iron-bearing clay which can be picked up in the desert. The skin was dipped six times in the dye mixed with iron.

After dyeing in any of these ways, the skin had to be twisted to dry it, then softened again. Burying it in the earth was the usual softening method. After being dug up, it was pulled, rubbed and stretched in the hands until it was soft and flexible. This rubbing treatment had to be repeated every time the skin got wet. No wonder the skin clothing was not washed much! Antelope hide, tougher and smaller than buckskin, was dressed in the same way.

108

Dressing Furry Skin. The skins of all furry animals, from fox to buffalo, were dressed with the hair on. This meant that only the flesh side was scraped. Then the skin was strewn with wood ashes and left for a few days, as a form of disinfecting, which would keep the hair from falling out later. If it was a thin, soft skin like those of fox, coyote, and wildcat, it might be rubbed with brains, but often the oil in the skin was enough. Then it was softened by rubbing and pulling with the hands, without soaking or twisting. Later on, sheep skin was treated in the same way. The tougher hides, like mountain lion and buffalo, were pounded. Mountain lion was first sprinkled with wood ashes. Buffalo, killed out on the Plains, was rubbed with some of the alkaline earth from dried ponds or buffalo wallows. It was carried home to break up the cells which would hold air and hasten decay. Between poundings, the worker rolled and pulled the tough hide in his hands to soften it. Finally he smoothed the hairless side by rubbing it with a piece of sandstone.

That was all they usually did to buffalo hide in the old days, pueblo people say. They did not paint it and they left the hair on, even when they were going to use it for moccasin soles. Hair wore off soon enough of itself. Later, when they began to use cowhide, they treated it in the same way and then sew it, hair side down, to the uppers of old shoes bought at white stores. When they used cowhide for moccasin soles, however, they began to dehair it like buckskin and lately they have blackened the upturned edges of the soles. The blacking is a paint, made from charcoal and soapweed (Yucca baccata in this case). Leaves of soapweed are laid over the fire until they are soft and wilted. Then they are twisted in the hands to wring out the juice. The sticky juice mixed with the powdered charcoal makes a hard shellac, which is painted on the upturned soles of the moccasins, making them shiny black against the rust red or dead white of the buckskin upper. We may remember that in painting basketry twigs earth colors were mixed with oil of sunflower seeds in much the same way.

Articles Made. Some skins were used whole. fox skins for the ceremonial costumes; large white buckskins for mantles; buffalo robes for bedding; smaller skins to sit on in the house. Most skins were cut up for bags or clothing, and even the whole ones went that way after they began to wear out. Beside leggings, moccasins, and shirts, men made an occasional cap out of a mountain lion's head or a bowguard of any strong skin on hand. The bags needed were mostly a case to keep the precious bow from getting wet, a quiver for arrows, or a sack for seed corn.

A man who had plenty of buckskin might make a long handsome bag to hold his bow, with fringes along one side or at the ends. The quiver was a smaller case sewed along the side of it. If he had time, he might decorate both with animal tails or smear colored clays over them. Sometimes a quiver was made of mountain lion or wildcat skin, sewed up along the stomach, the legs hanging down as a fringe and the head acting as a lid. The bag for seed corn was a small, soft fawn skin.

All men who went hunting or fighting made bowguards, to protect the left wrist from the kick of the bowstring. These were simply strips of tough leather—antelope or buffalo hide dyed black, or wildcat or mountain lion with the fur on. They were cut to fit the wrist and tied with a leather thong (V-3). After pueblo people learned silverwork from the whites, they sometimes added silver decoration. Some of the Tiwa made shields of buffalo hide, like the Plains Indians, and in that case they sometimes scraped the hair off. They cut the rawhide into a disk, perhaps two feet in diameter, and ran a strap through the center to hold it by. Then they laid it over warm ashes until it hardened like board. There were many other uses for skin, as in masks, anklets, and arm-bands, all parts of an elaborate ceremonial paraphernalia which is not described in this paper.

Skin Sewing. The sewing on bags and clothing was very simple. Perhaps it might be better called tying together with skin thongs. The edges of two pieces of skin were laid side by side, holes were made in them with a bone awl, and then the thong was pushed through and tied. Sometimes there were several holes and the thong was laced a little way. This was very different from the fine sewing with sinew done by some tribes, but pueblo people insist that the thongs were better. Sinew shrinks and stretches too much.

It was only in moccasin making that sinew thread was used, for footwear is not much good if there are long gaps between stitches. Every man kept a ball of sinew, from the various animals he had killed and probably old and hard as wood splinters, rolled up in his storeroom. When he wanted to use it he had to soak it, then split it with his teeth into threads. He used an awl for this sewing, too, for there seem to have been few American tribes except the Eskimo who sewed skin with needles. He had several awls, made from splinters of deer bone and rubbed to a point with sandstone. For moccasins he used a very fine awl and made holes which did not go all the way through the thick buckskin or buffalo hide, so that his stitches were invisible.

Mining

The pueblo were one of the few Indian groups which did any mining. Other tribes in the United States region broke off stone to make their tools, but without tunneling into the earth. Indians in the Lake Superior area quarried the native copper in this same way but the pueblo people dug as much as two hundred feet into the earth and for two substances: turquoise and coal.

Turquoise was what the miners sought oftenest, both to make their own jewelry, and to trade. Stones which seem to have come from the pueblo plateau are found in Mexico, and though we suppose the Mexicans must have had mines of their own, these have not yet been found. There are at least eight mines in pueblo country, most of them so valuable that they have been reworked by white people. The largest, at Cerillos, near Sante Fe, had a tunnel 200 feet deep and at some places the diggings are 300 or more feet wide. Another ancient tunnel goes thirty feet through solid granite and porphyry. The tools of the miners were only stone and bone. They evidently cracked the rock by fire, then hacked out pieces of it with stone hammers such as that on page 107. Finally they picked out the veins and nuggets of turquoise with picks of deerhorn. Sometimes the overhanging rock fell on the miners, as happened at the Cerillos mine in 1680. The bodies of the crushed Indians were found long afterward, fifty feet below the pit surface.

Early dwellers in pueblo country even went far afield after their turquoise. There are plenty of small deposits of the stone in the hot California desert known as the Mohave Sink. Here there are scraps of pottery and tools which show that some time before 800 A.D., people from pueblo country were camping in caves and mining turquoise in 200 different places. Evidently they did not stop to make jewelry on the spot but took the stones away and drilled at home.

The other kind of mining was for coal, and this was done by the Hopi alone. In fact, they were the only prehistoric coal miners in the United States. The dumps from their old tunnels can still be seen along the mesas and some are being opened again. From the tools found it looks as though the miners hacked into the coal seam with the long stone picks we mentioned (page 108), cracking out lumps which they broke up with a stone hammer. They tunneled into the mesa for twenty feet or so and perhaps carried the coal home in skin sacks. It is very soft, sub-bituminous and can hardly be used in a house because of its evil-smelling smoke. Probably it was used for pottery making, and some of the diggers guess that each woman may have had her own little mine.

There were salt mines, too, in Nevada and southern Arizona, but pueblo people seem to have got most of their salt from the deposits left by water at the lakes and springs where they made their sacred pilgrimages.

Jewelry

Pueblo men who brought home turquoise from the mines, sometimes made it into beads themselves and sometimes traded it to others who had skill in bead drilling. This was a delicate task, needing a special tool, and only a few men knew how to do it. Some, however, are using the old process to the present day, especially at Zuni. They chip a bit of turquoise or shell to about the right size and then drill a hole through it before shaping it into a

111

Plate V-6. Pump drill for making holes in turquoise

bead. Thus, if it cracks during the operation, there will not be so much work wasted.

The tool used is the pump drill. The plate V-6 shows this device which is a shaft of wood about one foot long with a sharp point fastened to the lower end. Once this point was a sliver of flint, but now it is metal, perhaps the tip of an old file. Some distance above the point there is a disk of wood, pottery, or stone, which acts as a flywheel to keep the shaft turning after it has been given a push. Above the disk and about half way along the length of the shaft is the device for pushing. It is a stick of heavy wood about two feet long, through the middle of which the shaft passes. We may call it the crosspiece. The ends of the crosspiece are attached to a long buckskin thong, just as the ends of a bow are attached to a bow string and the thong is threaded through a hole in the top of the shaft.

To start work the driller twirls the crosspiece around the shaft by hand, thus causing the two strings to twist tight around the rod and pulling the crosspiece up higher. The point of the shaft is on the bit of turquoise he wishes to drill and he holds it there with one hand. With the other he pushes down on the crosspiece. This untwists the strings and causes the shaft to whirl. The whirling does not stop when the strings are untwisted for the flywheel keeps the shaft going, thus twisting them up in the other direction. Now the driller pushes down on the crosspiece again and the whole operation is repeated. If he pushes gently and regularly the drill will work with almost the precision of a machine. Few Indians used such a complicated device as this though it used to be known in the Old World, before the days of machines. Perhaps the Spaniards brought it in early days but its history has long been forgotten.

The bead usually made is shaped like a small thick button about one sixty-fourth to three-eighths of an inch thick, and one sixteenth to one quarter of an inch in diameter. To shape the bits of turquoise or shell in this way the worker strings his drilled fragments on a string with a knot at one end. He pushes them tight against the knot, holding them down with his thumb and winding the extra string around his hand. Then he proceeds to shape them, first by knocking off rough edges with a hammer then by rolling his column of beads back and forth over a sandstone slab. He may roll them with his free hand or with another piece of sandstone, or he may knot the string at both ends, hold it upright and roll between two pieces of sandstone. The sandstone is kept wet and some grit is sprinkled on it, just as in the smoothing of stone for axes. When the column of beads has been rubbed long enough they are all of a size and shape, like a pile of the peppermints called Life Savers.

This work is easiest with beads of white clamshell which are already fairly smooth on the two flat sides, and need only drilling and rounding. Such beads are still worn by pueblo people and their neighbors, the Navaho. Some

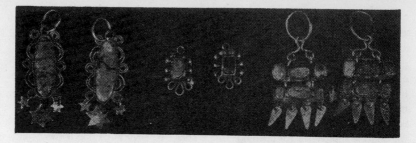

Plate V-7. Zuni silver and turquoise earrings

people mistakenly call them wampum, not realizing that wampum is a word used by the **Algonkins** on the Atlantic coast, for a bead which was cylindrical, not flat, and which served for records and for money. Turquoise beads are harder to make than shell for they need smoothing on the two flat sides. They are often larger than the white shell beads and sometimes oval, with the hole at one end. You often see such oval turquoise beads strung at intervals among white shell disks, in a very effective arrangement.

We have already spoken of the elaborate pendants found in the ancient pueblos. These were made by gluing chips of turquoise, jet or shell to flat pieces of wood or to abalone shell, with pinyon gum. Pueblo people continued to make such pendants and even now they are seen at dances. Simpler ones, made with modern materials, are peddled on the streets of Santa Fe.

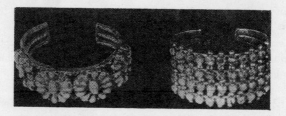

Plate V-8. Zuni silver and turquoise bracelets

Silver. After the whites came, pueblo people learned to use silver, perhaps as early as the Navaho did. No one knows the exact date but the latest guess is a little after 1850. Their material was coin silver, generally Mexican pesos, which they melted in a home-made crucible and hammered on a tiny forge, made in imitation of those they had seem among the whites. They stamped it with dies made from odd bits of old iron and one way to tell this old silver is that the designs are small and separate, each from a small die, instead of being grouped as they are when made from a complete modern die.

All the pueblos say they used to have silver workers—a surprise to those who think of this craft as Navaho specialty. They made the same objects as the Navaho: beads, buttons bracelets, bow guards, conchos, rings, and the horseshoe-shaped pendant, which, the students say, is an adaptation of the Spanish symbol to ward off the evil eye. One pueblo specialty was a little silver cross, never made by the unconverted Navaho. (Plate V-9)

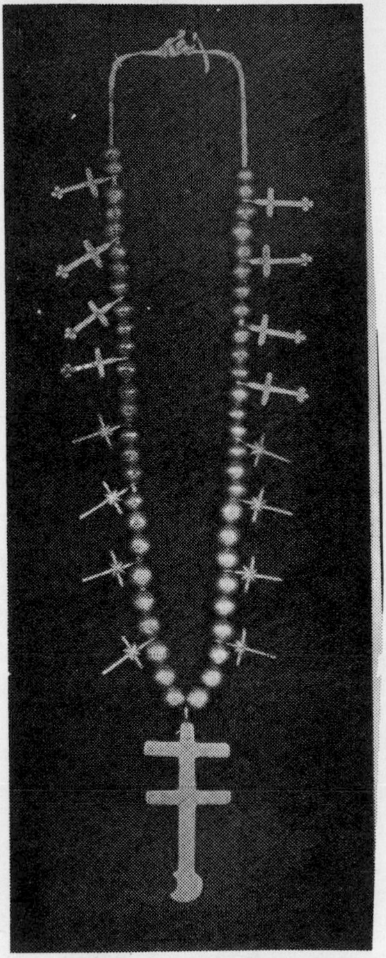

Zuni was the pueblo which car-·ied the art furthest and all experts :an recognize the rings and bracelets vhich come from there, made in deli-:ate openwork and loaded with tur-juoise in the old pueblo manner. Hopi began the work about 1890, aking its inspiration from Zuni. ately, its workers are developing an ndividual style with designs taken ·om their own basketry or pottery. ither pueblos started and stopped ut now almost all of them have one r more silversmiths making work for ale. Santo Domingo does a thriving ·ade.

The Arts and Crafts Board of the Department of the Interior is working ard to keep pueblo silver to a high tandard and to advertise it all over he country. It is to be hoped that, vhen white people appreciate this in-·eresting jewelry, pueblo families will not need to earn money by making lit-tle dolls out of commercial beads. For that is the situation today. It seems that the white tourist thinks all Indi-ans used beads, and the pueblos are Indians. It does not matter that they never did beadwork like the Plains Indians. They send to New York—or a trader sends—for bright colored beads made in Europe and whole families sit all day long making them into little dolls representing cowboys and Indians—just to satisfy the white tourists.

Plate V-9. Old silver necklace, Rio Grande pueblos

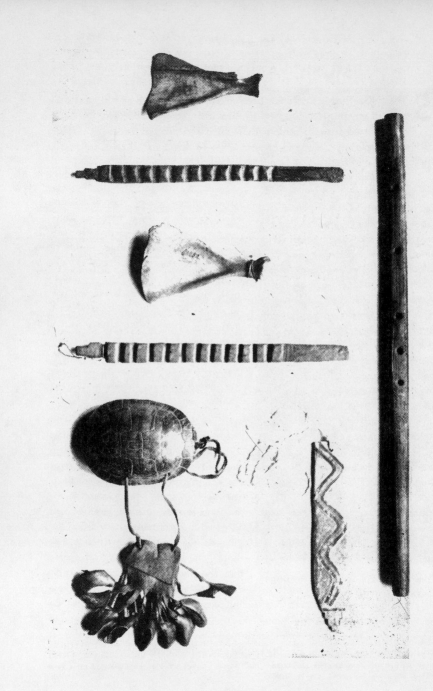

Chapter VI

MUSIC AND PAINTING

S INGING. Pueblo music has been said by one expert to be the most complex of any music among North American Indians. Doubtless the pueblos, a mixed group to begin with, learned and adopted the songs of many different peoples in the course of time. They turned them all to one purpose, the ceremonies which would bring supernatural help to crops and people.

Most of the music was furnished by chorus singing and anyone who has heard the subdued roar of men's voices as a file of dancers walks into the plaza knows how effective this is. The chorus does not sing parts. Like other American Indians, they all sing the air, with an occasional high note held by women singers. The distinguishing thing about this music is the variation of time. Each line of a song may be of different length. Instead of the regular, simple beat of white music, there will be a complicated beat, different for each measure. Indians feel that the rhythm of the white man's music, the same in every line, is too simple to be interesting.

The Rattle. Sometimes the singers or the men dancers accompany themselves with rattles. These are made of large gourds which grow wild in the Southwest and Mexico. Pueblo people sometimes raised them, both for dishes and for musical instruments. A man making a rattle chose a large pear shaped gourd with a long neck, perhaps an inch and a half thick. He cut off the tip of the neck and also the rough, short stem at the lower end of the squash, where the flower had withered off. This left a hole at each end, about an inch and a half in diameter. Perhaps at this time he pricked a pattern of holes in the soft sides of the gourd, using a sharp stick.

Now he might let it dry a little, until the meat and seeds inside became shrunken and loose. The current of air through the two holes kept them from rotting. Then he picked up a few small, sharp pebbles, poked them inside and, holding it by the ends, gave it a hard shaking. The pebbles broke the meat and seeds loose and finally he was able to dump them all out on the ground, leaving the inside as clean as a pot.

Now it must dry again. He plugged the bottom hole and filled the interior with sand, so it would keep a plump, even shape. After being left in the sun, its walls dried as hard as wood. Now it was ready for the pebbles which would make the rattling sound. These must be smooth and round, so that they would not cut the gourd. Hopi men picked them up from ant hills, for

◀

Plate VI-1. Pueblo musical instruments: rattle made of a single shoulder of deer; rattle made of tortoise shell with deer-hoofs attached to be worn behind the right knee in dance; notched stick, over which another stick is rubbed; "Bull-roarer," a flat piece of wood whirled on a long string, imitating the sound of rain; flute

the great black ants often make tall piles of stones, the size of small beads. Hopi and Zuni liked their pebbles to be of white quartz, or crystal. Some of the Rio Grande people liked them red.

The rattle maker placed a handful of pebbles inside the gourd. Then he stopped the holes by running a long stick through the gourd, so that it stuck out at both ends. At the bottom end, it stuck out only far enough to be fastened with pinyon gum. At the neck end, it extended four or five inches and provided a handle. If it had been well cut to size, it was just thick enough to fill the holes well. Then the gourd was painted. In former days, this was done with pottery clay in red or white, perhaps with figures. Now it is done with commercial dyes in striking colors. The brilliant rattle, its handle often decorated with feathers, is one of the most colorful parts of a dancer's costume.

Occasionally, in former days, rattles were made of buckskin in gourd shape. A hoop of green willow was made, as wide across as the desired rattle and a handle thrust through it, like a spear through a ring. The rattle maker took a piece of dressed skin from deer, antelope or mountain sheep. He dampened it, stretched it over hoop and handle, put some pebbles inside and let the skin dry into shape. It hardened so that the pebbles rattled against it almost as they did against a gourd.

Other rattles were made from the shell of the little land tortoise which walks about desert country. The animal was allowed to die and dry inside its shell and then was removed with pebbles like the meat of a gourd. The shells were supplied with pebbles, plugged and equipped with thongs so that they could be strapped just below a dancer's knee. (Plate VI-1) When a row of dancers raised their knees in unison, the rhythmical accompaniment came automatically. The dancers also tied bunches of antelope hoofs to their knees or their belts, or even to the tortoise sheel rattle. (Plate VI-1) In these days, they use sleigh bells.

The Notched Stick. Another form of rhythm was supplied by the notched stick. (Plate VI-1) This was a thin slab of wood, about eighteen inches long by two in diameter. One side was flattened and carved into transverse ridges, so that it looked like a narrow washboard. Those in the photograph also have handles at one end. The player knelt, placing one end of the stick on a gourd and holding the other in his left hand. In his right he held a shorter stick of smooth, hard wood, which he rubbed up and down against the ridges. This produced a harsh, loud scraping sound, longer and more penetrating than that of the rattle.

Usually the player made the sound louder by resting the lower end of the stick on an overturned basket or half of a gourd. The sound echoed through this as through a drum and perhaps this stick and gourd arrangement **was** the drum of early days. It is an instrument much used in Mexico

118

and also by the Papago and Pima, to the south of the pueblos. Pueblo people now use it only occasionally, in harvest dances. Generally the players are women, or men dressed as women, and they kneel, in their bright bordered shawls, facing a row of dancers.

The Drum. At present, the chief instrument for accompanying the dance is the drum. It is played by a drummer who stands at one side of a line of dancers or who walks along with a chorus. In former days, say old pueblo people, his drum was made of a large pot, partly filled with water and with a piece of deerskin tied tightly over its mouth. These old water drums give a fine, bell-like sound but only Zuni makes much use of them now. Drums in the other pueblos are made of a hollow cylinder of wood, with skin stretched over its open ends. No one is sure whether such a drum is an old pueblo instrument or whether it represents another case where some novelty, learned from whites or other Indians, has been cleverly adapted to pueblo needs and materials.

Pueblo people had a simple and practical way of getting the wooden cylinder. They looked for a fallen cottonwood or aspen log of the diameter they wanted, knowing that the soft wood inside would rot to powder, leaving a cylindrical shell. Men kept a lookout for such logs and a drum maker generally knew, months ahead, where he could find one. He cut off a section of the size he wanted and cleaned it well inside with a knife of stone or, later, of steel. Some pueblos liked their drums tall and those of the Tewa, for instance, may sometimes be used today as little tables. Others made them smaller like the old pot drum. In these days, many paint the outside of the wooden cylinder, often in bright turquoise blue. Pueblo people can usually tell where a drum was made by the size, color and workmanship. Cochiti, especially, excels in this art and sells drums throughout the Southwest.

The drum maker had been saving strong, thick pieces of buckskin for his drumheads. If he was lucky, he might have the tougher hide of antelope or mountain sheep or, best of all, buffalo. Today he uses horse or goat hide. Sometimes he dehaired the skin (see pages 112-116) but this was not necessary, since it would wear off as the drum was pounded. He never softened and dressed the skin, because a drumhead should be stiff.

He cut two pieces, much larger than the ends of the log over which they would fit. They were roughly circular but their edges were cut into points, to hold the lashing. He let them soak overnight, so they would stretch easily and, next day, fitted each over one end of the log, tying it temporarily in place. Then he punched holes in the points which extended down from each drumhead and laced the two heads together with a thong which passed back and forth along the length of the cylinder, tying the two skins together and pulling them tight. The wet skin dried in a shape which exactly fitted the ends of the drum. (Plate V-2)

119

Drummers carried this drum by a short rawhide loop at one side and, of course, never let it touch the ground. They beat it with a single drumstick, not two, such as the whites use. Sometimes they used a single headed drum, with skin stretched over a wooden hoop like a tambourine.

The Flute. The other pueblo instrument was the flute. (Plate VI-1) This was a rod of cottonwood or some soft wood which is pulpy inside. The maker cut a section two and a half to three feet long and punched out the pulpy inside with a hot wire. Pueblo people do not remember what he did before wires were to be had. He cut four holes in the further end. In the near end, he inserted a slanting mouthpiece of smooth wood, for this flute was blown from the end, not the side. Sometimes the flute was painted with the favorite turquoise blue of the pueblos and it might be decorated with feathers and strings of buckskin. Flutes of this sort would not play a tune and they were not used to accompany dancing or singing. The flute was a solo instrument, played by young men when they were courting. The Zuni used it in a corn grinding ceremony, when girls ground corn in unison while a young man played to them. The Hopi had two clans of Flute People, who performed a special ceremony, bringing rain to the mesas.

Painting. We have already spoken of the painting done on pottery which was the work of women and, in these days, of men too. There was other painting done by men on wooden properties for the altar and wooden head-dresses but their description would take us far into ceremony, which is not the province of this book. Men also painted murals.

Perhaps we could use the word murals about the ancient splotches in red and white found outside some of the ruined pueblos. They certainly were the prelude to mural painting and some of the sun symbols and rain clouds really take rank as pictures. These can be seen on hundreds of trails and roads in New Mexico wherever there is a smooth rock face near some old camp of pueblo people.

About fourteen or fifteen hundred A.D. (or earlier for all we know)

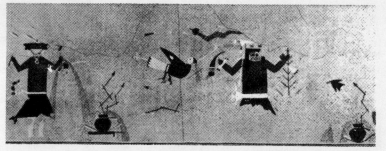

Plate VI-2. Kuaua murals, fragment of layer G-26, west wall

pueblo people began to paint pictures on the walls of the sacred rooms which we call kivas. First, they plastered the wall with smooth brown adobe, as was done in any house. Then they put on designs in the earth colors used for pottery—brownish red, yellow, white. These were mixed with water and, since they could not be fired, as the pottery was, they wore off in time. Then the artists would replaster the wall in brown and put on new designs. At Awatobi, a ruined village near the Hopi mesas, one wall had fifteen layers of such painting. At Kuaua (Kwa-waw), near Bernalillo, New Mexico, there were twenty-nine.

Modern students have done an amazing work in peeling off these layers glued to cloth and have preserved each one. When the pictures finally stood out, in their soft, earth colors, they revealed dancing figures like those seen in pueblo plazas today. The illustration (VI-2) shows one of these figures at the left, with kilt and white sash, mask and head feather. The bird at the center is a shape that still decorates pueblo pots. Plate VI-3 is a more formal design. Here a prehistoric Jemez artist has represented the arching rainbow and scalloped clouds which appear in pueblo ceremonies to this day. Guarding them are the horned water serpents, pueblo symbols of rain and blessing. Anyone who has seen Navaho sand paintings might almost mistake this for one of them. He will wonder again just when and how the newcomers

Plate VI-3. Kiva painting of the Jemez universe (pre-historic)

from the north began to use pueblo designs in working out an art of their own.

Ancient pueblo paintings were on walls or rock. There were no small movable ones until the white man brought paper. When this new material came, there was a sudden burst of activity such as often happens, when skilled workers have a chance at better tools. One day in 1910 white scientists noticed a San Ildefonso man drawing pictures on the smooth firm ends of a cardboard box. The picture (Plate VI-4) shows the kind of work done by one of these early artists, Alfredo Montoyo. It is the deer dance at San Ildefonso, with every detail clear as a jewel.

That was the pueblo style and it is to this day. We can see the careful drawings of feathers and embroidery, fine as a Persian miniature. We note there is no background, not even a line to show where sky and earth meet. The same is true of Russian icons and of Chinese scrolls. It was true of European paintings, too, some centuries ago. With pueblo paintings, the bright little figures always stand out in space with nothing to show in what world they move. They have no shadows. Nor does the artist measure space by making the figures smaller when they are far away. Look at the charming picture of the eagle dance by another of the early painters, Awa Tsireh of San Ildefonso. (Plate VI-5) All the singers are the same size, whether near us or not. If the colors could be shown, they would be equally bright, not melting into blue distance as they do with white paintings.

Plate VI-5. Eagle dance (Awa Tsireh)

Awa Tsireh was one of three pueblo boys taken into the employ of the School of American Research. They were not trained. The white scientists only gave them colors and time, hoping to see pueblo ideas flower in a new and different art. They were rewarded for all three artists are now famous. Plate VI-6 is a scene by the Hopi, Fred Kabotie, now teaching his

Plate VI-6. Little Pine ceremony (Fred Kabotie)

123

Plate VI-7. The Indian World (Ma-pi-wi)

Plate VI-8. Firing pueblo pottery (Ma-pi-wi)

Plate VI-9. Eagle dancers of Cochiti (Tonita Pena)

countrymen in an Indian school. We find that he has decided to use perspective in the white man's manner but his "Little Pine Dance" has the same brilliance, clearness, and dignity which belongs to all pueblo paintings. The next two illustrations (Plate VI-7 and VI-8) are by Velino Herrera, (Ma-pi-wi) of Zia pueblo. Ma-pi-wi has illustrated several books by this time and the cover of this volume shows how well. Visitors from all over the country are now having a chance to see his buffalo hunt and his dancing figures which seem to move in a world outside time and space, in a splendid mural which he completed in 1938, in the Department of the Interior at Washington, D. C.

Numbers of pueblo painters have followed these pioneers. If you visit San Ildefonso, (Plate VI-10) now the pueblo art center, you will be led to house after house where delicate water colors are propped against the white-washed wall. At the weekly market in Santa Fe the graceful shapes of antelopes, hunters, and dancers stand waiting for sale with the artists or their families smiling beside them. Some of the artists are women (Plate VI-9) who never painted human figures in the old days. That work, done in the kiva, was for men, while women never got far from the lines and angles of their pot designs. Now Tonita Peña and several others paint charming groups of bright shawled women, dancing, bringing food and making pottery. Pop Challee of Taos is famous for her leaping antelopes.

White experts have become aware of this new art. There have been exhibitions in New York, Chicago, even in Europe. Collectors are buying the paintings, and the young artist can now see a possibility never thought of before, that of really supporting himself by his art. Since 1933 the Santa Fe Indian School has had an art department and now Hopi High School at Oraibi has one. They are under Indian teachers who work to bring out the pueblo feeling for color, for accuracy, for dignity. For centuries this feeling has

125

Plate VI-10. Sun-buffalo dancer, San Ildefonso (Wo-peen)

been expressing itself in the arrangement of ceremonies, the painting of pottery and headdresses. Now it has further opportunities and a new style is being brought into American Art.

Chapter VII

THE CRAFTS TODAY

P UEBLO craft is continuing today but changing fast. One change is of a new kind, unknown in the pueblo history and it has taken place since the railroads brought cheap household goods. This is the dying out of many crafts as household necessities and their rebirth as skilled professions. Once every woman made pots and every man, in some pueblos, wove, for that was the only way to get kitchenware and clothing. Now these things can be bought so cheaply that no one would spend time producing them except for some special reason.

There are two such reasons. One is ceremony, which clings to the ancient things, hallowed by use. Every male dancer still wears a hand-woven kilt if he can get it. Many an altar has its handmade jar of spring water. A Hopi bridegroom receives his gift of cornmeal on a handmade basket tray. As the years go on and the villages grow more modern, perhaps these things will seem more important rather than less.

The other reason is sale. We have seen that the pueblos always traded and, perhaps, their craft workers made a specially beautiful article now and then, with the hope of getting some luxury from other Indians in exchange. But also they made their own equipment and had to. Now, no one has to. So the workers who did not care for craft or had no skill with it, have dropped out. Those who continue are the specially skilled ones, who can get a good price. It is the same thing that has happened all over the world, as one country after another got access to machine-made goods. Irish linen and Scotch tweed, once made for the home, are now for sale and perhaps not used by the people who produce them. Still, they are famous and have been for decades. Perhaps the pueblo crafts, after their new turn, will have a like history.

At present, they are in all stages of change. Weaving is still done mostly for ceremony and sold to other Indians or, perhaps, traded in the old way. Winnowing baskets and plain cooking ware are still made by many women for their own use. Decorated pottery, however, is made for sale and the buyers are the whites. This art has made the complete change from a household necessity to a money making profession. Others, like embroidery, silverwork, or drum making were never necessities, and perhaps, in former days, they were only done by a few people though not for pay. Now they are becoming money makers. Painting on paper, the new profession, was paid work from the start.

Few people devote full time to such work. Almost all carry on house work or farming as well and some may work only a few hours a week. Others make most of their living from craft and produce in quantities never heard of in the old days. This means they have much more time for skill and originality. No Indian yet manufactures in standard lots. Each article is different and each one gets personal attention. The woman who makes two hundred pots a year has time to perfect herself as her grandmother never could in making ten. She can be tempted, of course, to turn out careless work which will sell quickly and the temptation is great. Or, she may use her energy and imagination to work up new styles.

Sales will decide the results, for only an unusual woman can take time for good pots when the average buyer wants twenty-five cent ash trays. So the pressing question for Indian craft today is the method of sale. So far, there is no standard arrangement. Tewa villages, like San Ildefonso and Santa Clara are so famous the people come there in sightseeing busses to visit the houses or to find the pots spread out in the plaza. Santo Domingo, Laguna and Acoma build little booths along the motor highways where tourists from all States in the Union whirl past. Many pueblo people take a sack of pots or a pile of rugs over their shoulders and go to the nearest trading store where they sell their work outright, letting the trader wait for customers. Usually the trader is a white man, since he needs a white man's capital and business knowledge. However, there are a few Indian traders and, as the schools provide advanced business training, their number may increase.

White people, too, feel some responsibility about Indian craft, since they are the purchasers. It is a general impression that white influence puts an end to Indian craft, or at least true Indian craft, but this is not always true. Silverwork, in the pueblos, began when the whites brought new materials and tools. Weaving took a new spurt. Pottery died down and was reborn after the coming of the railroads. Its new form, as a skilled profession, was due to Indians nourished by white appreciation. The two most famous potters, Nampeyo of Hopi First Mesa and Maria Martinez, of San Ildefonso, got their first encouragement from white museum workers. If these students had not been interested in seeing the forgotten pottery revived and in finding purchasers, even such talented women could hardly have devoted their lives to it.

Now, several white groups are helping the craft movement along its new road. They have two aims. One is to help the Indians in their search for the most beautiful designs used throughout the centuries. The other is to educate white buyers, so they will appreciate such designs. It is not so simple as might be thought for an Indian craft worker to know about the art of her own people. Suppose she is a potter. There may have been no potters in her family or, perhaps, in her whole village for a generation. Or there may have been a period of poor design after the new, cheap goods came in. She might have a hard time finding out about the beautiful things in her own native

128

tradition were it not for the museums. For white collectors have been buying up the pots since 1879 and now there are more good ones in a museum than in almost any village.

The Indians go to see them and they ask questions. They get explanations of the sketches and notes which the whites have had time and money to make while the Indians have not. People of the river pueblos go to the New Mexico State Historical Museum and the Laboratory of Anthropology, at Santa Fe. They find friends in the New Mexico Association for Indian Affairs which gives prizes to each pottery-making pueblo every year for the best pots, new style and old style. The Hopi find a craft center in the Museum of Northern Arizona at Flagstaff.

The white groups can help with craft selling now and then or even with an engagement to demonstrate. They have, besides, the task of showing White Americans, all over the country, what good pueblo art really is. The museums send out exhibitions and printed material. The New Mexico Association for Indian Affairs advertises a weekly sale of pueblo craft in the Santa Fe plaza, with craft workers from a different pueblo every week. On Saturday mornings in summer the portico before the old governor's palace is gay with their bright shirts and shawls. White tourists pick their way among pots in shiny black or red, pottery animals, drums, bows, and arrows or string of colored corn, bright as jewels. No traveler returns to his home State without talking about the Indian market at Santa Fe.

The Indian Bureau has a special responsibility. Part of it touches the boarding schools, where some young people spend their time when they might be learning crafts at home. So weaving, silverwork, embroidery, leather work are taught under native teachers. Pottery, it turns out, can be better learned at home. The school of painting at Santa Fe is famous for a style that belongs to Southwest Indians and to no one else. Its exhibitions have gone to most of the great museums of the United States and even to Europe. There is a salesroom for all these arts at the Santa Fe school.

The Indian Bureau works, too, through the Indian Arts and Crafts Board of the Department of the Interior. The Board is a recent one and its aim is to do for Indian craft all over the country what local groups are doing in the Southwest. This means to help guide the crafts workers in their new career as skilled professionals and to find them a market. Perhaps, when enough time and energy have been put into this, we may see one craft after another reborn to take its place as part of the permanent artistic wealth of America.

FURTHER READING ON PUEBLO CRAFTS

T HIS list gives only detailed descriptions of craft work. There are many references to craft in more general books but these are given in the reading list of another volume, WORKADAY LIFE OF THE PUEBLOS.

ABBREVIATIONS

The initials for the institution issuing the publication are first given, with the address where publications can be obtained. Indented beneath it are the initials for its various publications, as B—Bulletin, M—Memoir, etc.

AA
American Anthropologist. Published at Menasha, Wis. Back numbers from Miss Bella Weitzner, American Museum of Natural History, New York, N.Y. A technical quarterly, usually without illustrations.

AAA
American Anthropological Association. Treasurer, from whom publications are ordered: Miss Bella Weitzner. See above.

—M
Memoirs. Material similar to that in the Anthropologist but in longer pamphlet form.

AMNH
American Museum of Natural History, New York, N. Y.

—AP
Anthropological Papers. Technical pamphlets, sometimes with plates.

BAE
Bureau of American Ethnology, Washington, D. C. Some publications of the Bureau are out of print but may be obtained from such dealers as Dauber and Pyne, Washington, D. C., Schulte, Fourth Ave., New York.

—R
Report. A series of elaborate, illustrated volumes, issued yearly from 1880-1929.

—B
Bulletin. Smaller volumes, few illustrations. These include many of the Bureau's publications on archaeology and music.

CU
Columbia University, New York. Publications from the Columbia University Press, New York City.

—CA
Contributions to Anthropology. Full volumes reporting anthropological field work.

EP
El Palacio. Small sized monthly with popular articles and photographs.

DAM
Denver Art Museum, Denver, Colo.

—L
Leaflets, of three or four pages and a good photograph. Each contains a simplified digest of material on some phase of Indian life. Excellent for purchase and distribution in a school.

—AS   Field Columbian Museum, Chicago, Ill.

FCM   Anthropological Series. Full volumes reporting anthropological field work. Technical, few illustrations.

HSNM —PH   Historical Society of New Mexico. Publications in History, State Museum, Santa Fe, N.M. Pamphlets by historical experts. A few illustrations.

LA   Laboratory of Anthropology, Santa Fe, N.M.

—M   Memoirs. Volumes on special phases of pueblo art with fine colored illustrations.

MNAI   Museum of the North American Indian (Heye Foundation), New York, N. Y.

—NM   Notes and Monographs. Small sized volumes, with detailed description of crafts.

MNM   Museum of New Mexico, Santa Fe, N. M.

MNA   Museum of Northern Arizona, Flagstaff, Ariz.

—MN   Museum Notes. Small leaflets, usually unillustrated but giving valuable practical information from workers in archaeology and crafts in the Hopi area.

—P   Plateau, an illustrated quarterly, successor to Museum Notes.

—B   Bulletin. Pamphlets in the manner of Museum Notes but longer.

NGM   National Geographic Magazine, Washington, D. C. Illustrated popular material.

NMHR   New Mexico Historical Review, State Museum, Santa Fe, N. M. A quarterly giving authoritative articles on New Mexican history. Unillustrated.

PMCM   Public Museum of the City of Milwaukee, Wis.

—B   Bulletin. Illustrated pamphlets.

SWM   Southwest Museum, Highland Park, Los Angeles, Calif.

—L   Leaflet. Small sized, illustrated pamphlets.

—P   Papers. Larger pamphlets.

        Frederic Webb Hodge Memorial Fund. A series of larger illustrated pamphlets.

ScM   Scientific Monthly, Science Press, Lancaster, Penn. The monthly publication of the American Association for the Advancement of Science. Authoritative articles on varied scientific subjects, usually not too detailed for the layman.

        Smithsonian Institution, Washington, D. C.

—R   Report.

MC   Miscellaneous Collections.

-P   Publications. These volumes are to be found only in larger and more specialized libraries and many are out of print. They give valuable information by museum collectors from 1870 on, with photographs and sketches.

TRB   Tree Ring Bulletin, Tucson, Ariz.

UC   University of Chicago Press, Chicago, Ill.

---PA   Publications in Anthropology. Full sized volumes reporting field work.

USNM   United States National Museum, Washington, D. C.

---AR   Annual Report.

---P   Proceedings.

UNM   University of New Mexico Press, Albuquerque, N. M.

---B   Bulletin.

---ES   Ethnobiological Series. Both of the above are small sized, technical pamphlets with no illustrations.

YU   Yale University, New Haven, Conn.

---PA   Publications in Anthropology. Large sized pamphlets reporting field work. No illustrations.

CSA   General Series in Anthropology, Menasha, Wis. Technical subjects, no illustrations.

GENERAL

McGregor, John C.

Southwestern Archaeology.

John Wiley and Sons, New York, 1941.

This is the most recent and complete statement on the subject. Meant for college classes, the book gives a clear, factual account of each of the village groups in the Southwest with the equipment which they manufactured at different stages. Houses, tools and pottery are amply illustrated. Excellent bibliographies for those who want further reading on archaeology.

Colton, H. S.

Stages in Arizona Prehistory.

MNA—MN. Vol. 8, No. 1

Brief summary with table placing the different crafts.

Bartlett, Katherine

Life in Pueblo II.

MNA—MN. Vol. 6, No. 3

Brief description of food, dress, crafts, etc., at a time a little later than the above.

Gifford, E. W.

Culture Element Distributions, XII Apache-Pueblo.

UC—AR 4:1, 1940.

This publication, of an entirely different sort from the others, lists a long array of "traits" concerned with crafts and customs, marking each present or absent. A valuable reference work in connection with other material. Walpi (Hopi) is one of four pueblos treated.

BASKETRY

GENERAL

Bartlett, Katherine
How to Appreciate Hopi Handcrafts.
MNA—MN, Vol. 9, No. 1.

Colton, Mary Russel F.
Technique of the Major Hopi Crafts.
MNA—MN, Vol. 3, No. 12.
The Hopi Craftsman
MNA—MN. Vol. 3, No. 1.

Douglas, Frederic H.
Basketry Construction Techniques.
DAM—L 67 1935.
Southwestern Twined, Wicker and Plaited Basketry.
DAM—L 99, 100 1940.

Hough, Walter
The Hopi Indian Collection in the U. S. National Museum.
USNM, Proceedings, Vol. 54 1919.
Pictures and descriptions of basketry articles.

HOPI

Jeancon, Jean and Douglas, Frederic H.
Hopi Indian Basketry.
DAM—L 17 1930.

Mason, Otis T.
Aboriginal American Basketry.
U. S. National Museum, Annual Report, 1902.

Weltfisch, Gene
Prehistoric North American Basketry Techniques and Modern Distributions.
AA, Vol. 32, No. 3, 1934.

JEMEZ

Stevenson, James
Illustrated catalogue of the collections obtained from the Indians of New Mexico.
BAE—R, 2, 1880-81.
Good pictures of the basket on pages 370 and 391.

Williamson, Ten Broeck
The Jemez Yucca Ring Basket.
EL Palacio, Vol. XLII, Nos. 7, 8, 9, 1937.

WEAVING

Colton, Mary Russel F

The Arts and Crafts of the Hopi Indians.
MNA—MN, Vol. 11, No. 1
Technique of the Major Hopi Crafts.
MNA—MN, Vol. 3, No. 12
The Hopi Craftsman.
MNA—MN, Vol. 3, No. 1
Wool for Our Indian Weavers, What Shall It Be?
MNA—MN, Vol. 4, No. 12

Douglas, Frederic H.

1. Main Types of Pueblo Cotton Textiles.
DAM—L, 92-93. 1940.
2. Indian Cloth Making.
DAM—L, 59-60. 1937.
3. Main Types of Pueblo Woolen Textiles.
DAM—L, 94-95. 1940.
Hopi Indian Weaving.
DAM—L, 18. 1930.
Weaving at Zuni Pueblo.
DAM—L, 96-97. 1940.
Weaving in the Keres Pueblos and in the Tiwa Pueblos and Jemez.
DAM—L, 91. 1939.
Acoma Pueblo Weaving and Embroidery.
DAM—L, 89. 1939.
Weaving in the Tewa Pueblos.
DAM—L, 90. 1939.

The above form a useful summary of the subject, with photographs many of which the author has kindly allowed us to reproduce here.

Notes on Hopi Brocading.
MNA—MN, Vol. 11, No. 4, 1931.

This is a detailed description of brocading or embroidery weaving which could be used by a weaver.

Lewton, Frederic L.

The Cotton of the Hopi Indians: A New Species of Gossypium.
SI—MC, LX, 1913.

Kent, Kate Peck

The Braiding of a Hopi Wedding Sash.
MNA—P, Jan. 1940.

A careful step-by-step description of this intricate process with diagrams, some of which are reproduced in this book.

Notes on the Weaving of Prehistoric Textiles.
MNA—P, Vol. 14, No. 1, July 1941.

An excellent summary of all that is known on the pueblos, with diagrams and lists of specimens.

MacLeish, Kenneth
>**Notes on Hopi Belt Weaving at Moenkopi.**
>AA, Vol. 42, No. 2. 1940.
>Valuable detailed description with diagrams.

Mason, O. T.
>**A Primitive Weaving Frame.**
>USNM—R, 1899.
>Description of the reed heddle used on the belt loom.

Speir, Leslie
>**Zuni Weaving Technique.**
>AA, Vol. 26, No. 1, 1924.
>A careful description with diagrams which will serve for all pueblos. Includes both blanket and waist looms.
>**Zuni Weaving.**
>EP, 1924, Vol. 16, No. 12.

Stevenson, James
>**Illustrated Catalogue of the Collections Obtained from the Indians of New Mexico.**
>BAE—R, No. 2, 1880-81.
>This catalogue, useful for reference on all pueblo handicrafts, contains fine colored pictures of Hopi textiles as well as drawing of a weaver, opp. p. 455.

BOOKS ON NAVAHO WEAVING USEFUL FOR REFERENCE

Some of the most thorough descriptions of Southwest weaving have been written about the Navaho who learned weaving from the pueblos and whose practice resembles theirs at most points. The most useful of these are:

Amsden, Charles
>**Navaho Weaving, Its Technic and History.**
>Fine Arts Press, Santa Ana, Calif. 1934.
>Clear description of every process with illustrations. Many specific mentions of pueblo weaving.

Matthews, Washington
>**Navaho Weavers.**
>BAE—R, No. 3, 1884.
>The first good description of Southwest weaving mentioning and illustrating the pueblos as well as Navaho.

Reichard, Gladys A.
>**The Navaho Shepherd and Weaver.**
>J. J. Augustin, New York, 1936.
>A manual for weavers, referring specifically to the Navaho but with good practical information on many processes common to Navaho and pueblos.

Bunzel, Ruth L.

The Pueblo Potter: A Study of Creative Imagination in Indian Art.
C. U. Press, 1920.

Many plates and figures. Critical comparison of styles at Zuni, Acoma, Hopi, San Ildefonso, with a history of their development.

Chapman, Kenneth

The Pottery of Santo Domingo Pueblo.
LA—M. Vol. 1, 1936.

A wealth of colored plates.

Symmetry of Pueblo Pottery Shapes.
EP, 1924, Vol. 16, No. 11.

Pueblo Feather Designs.
EP, 1927, Vol. 23, No. 1.

Zuni Bird Designs.
EP, 1928, Vol. 24, No. 2.

Brief articles by an authority. Illustrations.

Douglas, Frederic H.

Pottery of the Southwestern Tribes.
DAM—L, 69-70. 1935.

Modern Pueblo Pottery Types.
DAM—L, 53-54. 1935.

Brief summaries with photographs.

Guthe, Carl

Pueblo Pottery Making.
Philips Academy, Andover, Massachusetts, 1925.

Factual description of coiling, polishing, firing, as carried out at San Ildefonso. Pictures.

Jeancon, Jean A.

Santa Clara and San Juan Pottery.
DAM—L, 35. 1931.

Jeancon, Jean and Douglas, Frederic H.

Hopi Indian Pottery.
DAM—L, 47. 1932.

Pueblo Indian Pottery Making.
DAM—L, 6. 1935.

Brief summaries with photographs.

Mera, H. P.

**Style Trends of Pueblo Pottery in the Rio Grande and Little Colorado
Areas from the 16th to the 19th Century.**
LA—M, Vol. 11, 1939.

Interesting discussion with many plates.

The Rainbird: A Study in Pueblo Design.
LA—M, Vol. 2, 1937.

Almost entirely plates in color. Excellent material for exhibition or for an art class.

COLORED PLATES AND DRAWINGS OF POTTERY
IN MUSEUM CATALOGUES

The references given below have little descriptive text but provide fine pictures, not otherwise obtainable, for reference and exhibition.

Fewkes, Jesse Walter

Archaeological Expedition to Arizona in 1895.
BAE—R 17, pt. 2.
The Sikyatki pottery which gave the inspiration to modern Hopi.
Designs on Prehistoric Hopi Pottery.
BAE—R 33, 1911-12.
Two Summers Work in Pueblo Ruins.
BAE—R 22, pt. 1. 1900-1901.
Prehistory Hopi pots as well as others farther south.

Holmes, William H.

Pottery of the Ancient Pueblos.
BAE, 4, 1882-83 (Prehistoric Pottery).

Stevenson, James

Collections From New Mexico.
BAE—R 2, 1800-1881, Contemporary pottery.

JEWELRY

Blake, William P.

Mosaics of Chalcuite.
American Antiquarian, Vol. 22, No. 2, 1900.

Colton, Mary Russel F.

Hopi Silversmithing, Its Background and Future.
MNA—MN, Vol. 12, No. 1.

Jeancon, Jean A.

Pueblo Shell Beads and Inlay.
DAM—L 30. 1931.

TOOLS AND WEAPONS

Hough, Walter

Stone Working at Tewa.
AA, Vol. 10, No. 6, 1890.
Pictures of tools and weapons in museum collections listed in USNM—P, Vol. 54, BAR —R 2, opp. p. 375.

Mason, C. T.

North American Bows, Arrows and Quivers.
Smithsonian Publication, 962, 1895.
A general discussion with some information on the pueblos.

McGuire

A Study of the Primitive Methods of Drilling.
USNM—AR, 1894.

Colored picture of a pump drill in use, opp. p. 118.

Rogers, Spencer L.

The Aboriginal Bow and Arrow of North America and Eastern Asia.
AA, Vol. 42, No. 2, 1940.

MINING

Ball, Sidney H.

The Mining of Gems and Ornamental Stones by American Indians.
BAE—B No. 128, 1941.

Bartlett, Katherine

Prehistoric Mining in the Southwest (with map).
MNA—MN, Vol. 7, No. 10.

Blake, William P.

Aboriginal Turquoise Mining in Arizona and New Mexico.
American Antiquarian, Vol. 21, No. 5, 1899.

Brew, J. O. and Hack, John T.

Prehistoric Use of Coal by Indians of Northern Arizona.
MNA—P, July 1939.

PAINTING

Exposition of Indian Tribal Arts

Leaflet, 4 pages, magazine size, with photographs of modern Indian paintings. Copies from Laboratory of Anthropology, Santa Fe, New Mexico.

d'Harnoncourt, Rene and Douglas, F. H.

Indian Art of the United States.
New York, Museum of Modern Art, 1941.

Fine photographs of pueblo painting as well as of other arts, with brief descriptive text.

Hewett, Edgar L.

Pre-Hispanic Frescoes in the Rio Grande Valley.

POETRY

Bunzel, Ru+h

Zuni Ritual Poetry.
BAE—R 47, 1929.

Free poetic translations.

Spinden, Joseph H.

Songs of the Tewa, (Translated).
Exposition of Indian Tribal Arts, New York, 1933.

Copies now obtainable from Laboratory of Anthropology, Santa Fe, New Mexico.

Walton, E. L. and Waterman, T. T.
   American Indian Poetry.
   AA, XXVIII, 1925.

MUSIC

Bailey, Virginia
   Indian Music of the Southwest.
   EP, Vol. VLIV, Nos. 1 and 2.
   A brief introductory statement, quoting several songs with music.

Densmore, Frances
   The Music of Santo Domingo Pueblo.
   SWM—P. 1938.
   The music of many songs with analysis and some description.

Herzog, George
   A Comparison of Pueblo and Pima Musical Styles.
   AFL—J, Vol. 49, No. 144, 1936.
   An interesting paper for those with some musical knowledge.

Roberts, Helen
   Chakwena Songs of Zuni and Laguna.
   AFL—J 36, 1923.
   Transcription and discussion of the music of several songs.

Plate VI-11. Dancer and drummer from mural in Department of the Interior, Washington, D. C.
(Ma-pi-wi)